# MR. MUSTARD PLASTER
## AND OTHER MORMON ESSAYS

# MR. MUSTARD PLASTER
## AND OTHER MORMON ESSAYS

# MARY
# LYTHGOE
# BRADFORD

GREG KOFFORD BOOKS
SALT LAKE CITY, 2015

Copyright © 2015 Mary Lythgoe Bradford
Cover design copyright © 2015 Greg Kofford Books, Inc.
Cover design by Thayne Whiting

Published in the USA.

Greg Kofford Books
P.O. Box 1362
Draper, UT 84020
www.gregkofford.com
facebook.com/gkbooks

Also available in ebook.

2019     18     17     16     15     5     4     3     2     1

Library of Congress Cataloging-in-Publication Data
available upon request.

*This book is dedicated to my families,*
*who aided and abetted me and*
*acted as my cast of characters:*
*My deceased husband, my three children;*
*my parents, and my brothers and my sister.*

# CONTENTS

Introduction                                               ix

Foreword—I, Eye, Aye: A Personal Essay
    on Personal Essays                 xi

## I. LEAVING HOME

Yesterday the Wardhouse                                     3

Mr. Mustard Plaster                                         9

An Art Deco Childhood                                      13

Girl of the Limberlost and Lonesome Pine                   17

Virginia Sorensen: A Saving Remnant                        21

## II. SETTLING IN

Marriage and Printmaking                                   33

Seeding In                                                 39

My Christmas Disasters                                     45

Diet Dialogue                                              49

The Hourglass Factor                                       53

Pillows of My Faith                                        59

## III. MOVING ON

The Diary Chain                                            67

The Veil                                                   73

Gentle Dad                                                 79

Surprise Party: Meditations on Aging                       91

The Walking Cure                                           97

## IV. REACHING OUT

| | |
|---|---|
| Across the Generations | 105 |
| This Precious Stone | 109 |
| My Ten-Day Mission | 117 |
| A Ten-Day Expert Speaks | 133 |
| As We Rode Out One Late Summer Morning | 137 |

## V. HANGING ON

| | |
|---|---|
| Suddenly Single | 153 |
| It Takes Many Villages | 163 |
| Sweet Home: An Epilogue | 171 |
| Afterword: "They Also Serve" (Who Only Sit and Write) | 175 |

# INTRODUCTION

This collection of essays is the closest I can come to an autobiography. The personal essay is important to me, not only as the quintessential Mormon genre but also as a form suitable to my memories, thoughts, and wanderings. I don't pretend to have perfected it. When Eugene England first talked me into trying my hand at it in the late 1960s, the essay was not as prevalent in Mormon or American literature as it is now. At the time, Gene, in his role as editor of *Dialogue: A Journal of Mormon Thought,* made a distinction betweeen the ordinary essay, the kind we must all write at school, and the personal essay, which is as eccentric and as individual as the writer herself. Gene instigated a regular section called "Personal Voices," to which I contributed under the heading "Leaving Utah." Since then I have written intermittently for *Dialogue* and other publications and have edited the essays of others. When Sue Booth-Forbes gave me an opportunity to write a column called "A Woman's Perspective" for *Exponent II,* I welcomed it. Writing helps to clarify my life.

This collection is organized loosely in five sections related to phases of my life and their recurring themes. When I see them collected, I find that certain experiences repeat themselves as I look at them from the different contexts in my life. I have included a more or less scholarly essay on Virginia Sorensen because my graduate work is an important part of my background.

Since my life is still being lived, I think of this as a journey, not a product but a process.

This collection was first published by Signature Books in 1987 when it was awarded the Best Essay Award by the Mormon Letters Association. I am indebted to friends at the now defunct Greentree Publishing, Ellie and Sterling Colton, who helped prepare the manuscript and to Dixie Barlow, my astute editor. I thank the editors of *Dialogue, Exponent II,* and *Sunstone,* past and present, for first publishing me.

The present volume was suggested and edited by my publication guru, Brent Corcoran, and copy editors Lavina Fielding Anderson and Jani Fleet.

# I, EYE, AYE:
# A PERSONAL ESSAY ON
# PERSONAL ESSAYS

## I

In *A Believing People,* Richard Cracroft and Neal Lambert lament that the essay "has not been as vital a literary force in Mormondom as might be expected." Early Mormons, they note, kept forceful diaries, wrote poetry (much of it didactic), recorded their sermons, eschewed fiction, but what passed for essays "read like editorials" and avoided the revelation of personal feelings and attitudes:

> The personal essay with all of its reflection and scrutiny on life, seemed to have little role in Mormon literature, although the personal reminiscences of the pioneer and the General Authority were—and still are—important. As the church struggled for its corporate life, its members saw more value in writing of those things which fostered group identity than they did in examining those individual characteristics which make each Saint different from his brother.[1]

I don't know why we expected early Mormons to write essays. I am not surprised that they didn't. They were too busy pushing back frontiers and building monuments. They might have turned parts of their diaries into essays, but essays are usually written in tranquility, and in those early days there was little tranquility in Mormon life—nor is there much today. The busy structure of the modern church does not lend itself to the rumination required for the birth of that fragile form—the personal essay.

Nor do I think essays can grow from the soil of Mormon life without considerable husbanding. They must be cultivated like the plants that transformed the desert. Both readers and writers must help create the right environment for the growth of this distinctive form which is capable of giving such peculiar and particular pleasure.

"Peculiar and particular"—these are the words to describe the personal essay. I think of Lowell Bennion rubbing his chin as he ponders the possibility of being both rationally and emotionally committed to his faith; I think of Eugene England blessing his Chevrolet and of Laurel Thatcher Ulrich marching bravely into priesthood meeting to tell the brethren how it feels to be a woman; I see Ed Geary saying goodbye to his hometown; I see Dean May irrigating his garden, Clifton Jolley watching for his baby's first smile. I see peculiar people setting down their particular observations according to their own slightly eccentric habits, and I celebrate their truthfulness, their willingness to risk themselves for small gain. I celebrate them for their willingness to be vulnerable, for the personal essay is vulnerable. It cannot stand upon its footnotes.

I first became aware of the personal essay in Mormon life through the writings of Parley A. Christensen. He was still teaching at Brigham Young University when I went there as an instructor more than thirty years ago. I am glad to have known him in his last years and to have been introduced to his *All in a Teacher's Day: Essays of a Mormon Professor* (Salt Lake City: Stevens & Wallace, Inc., 1948). His was a calm and witty dedication to the humanities and to the teaching of the humanities.[2]

My real commitment to the form began, however, with the founding of *Dialogue: A Journal of Mormon Thought* in 1966. Its editors, especially Gene England, were devoted to the essay as a logical extension of that vital form—the testimony. The first issue carried what I believe to be one of the finest essays ever written by a Mormon—"The Challenge of Honesty" by Frances Lee Menlove.[2] Who, having read that first issue, can forget the "myth of the unruffled Mormon" and the "malaise among Mormons today" which keeps them from confronting their own "inner reality" and dealing openly with what they do and do not believe?

The mid-1960s also saw published Karl Keller's "Every Soul Has Its South," a moving account of a Mormon's venture into the civil rights movement:

"You leave God behind, you know, when you enter Kentucky," the driver of the car said as we crossed the Ohio River bridges into Louisville. "This is the South, the damned and damning South."

I was a Mormon going civil-rights-ing and that made a difference. Local members advised me not to go. It's not approved. You're needed here, it's beneath you; you can't change things. . . . you're not the type; but little did they know the reasons of the blood.[3]

In 1967 Carlos Whiting wrote his popular conversion essay, "An Honorable Surrender" (followed in 1974 by "Some Thoughts on a Rational Approach to Mormonism"). Conversion came to him "suddenly," he wrote:

There was no voice and no vision. I merely surrendered, as the honest and honorable thing to do. It was a Sunday morning and we were at breakfast. In a few minutes my family and I would leave for Sunday School at a nearby protestant church. There was a notable unwillingness to go (I was an officer and had many responsibilities in the church and it was my duty to attend). I looked around the table at my wife and young children.

"Should we go to Mormon Sunday School?" I surprised us all by asking.

"Yes, let's," they clamored.

I smiled wryly at my wife. "I'm converted at the breakfast table."[4]

Others followed, most notably Carole Hansen's "Death of a Son," an eloquent and painful account of a child dying of cancer, the inability of the elders to heal him and an ensuing renewal of faith.[5] By 1971 such personal essays, under the title "Personal Voices," had become a regular *Dialogue* feature. In this space Victor Cline, whose fine "The Faith of a Psychologist" appeared in *Dialogue*'s first issue, regularly contributed his fascinating and, to some readers, maddening opinions. Lowell Bennion shared his thoughtful reflections on the meaning of daily life, and Ed Geary perfected his brilliant predilection for the nostalgic yet unsentimental that has become a mainstay of the genre.[6]

Happily the fresh pace of the late 1960s accelerated in the 1970s. The "pink" woman's issue of summer 1971 helped launch the now well-established *Exponent II,* published originally by Claudia L. Bushman et al., and carried on by Nancy Dredge and Grethe B. Peterson in Boston (and, since this essay was written, by Susan E. Howe and Sue Paxman). In that issue Laurel Thatcher Ulrich debuted as an essayist in a personal discussion on birth control; Christine Meaders Durham debuted in an account of how she and her husband not only raised babies but also put each other through school. Lucybeth Rampton's Mother's Day speech qualifies as a fine personal document. Such essays as Almera Anderson Romney's prize-winning account of life as a white teacher in a black school, "All Children are Alike Unto Me," joined Jaroldeen Edwards's hymn to the earth mother, in "Full House":

> I wake up in the morning to the sound of my husband's voice. But it is not really an awakening, rather it is a continuing. For night as we used to know it no longer comes to our home. There is a lull in activity, yes; but in the way of our youth, when night and sleep were a total experience that blocked the chain of day's, a precious all-in-one piece of unconsciousness, an ending and a forgetting—in that sense night does not come.[7]

*BYU Studies, Exponent II, Sunstone,* the BYU alumni publication *BYU Today* (now *Brigham Young Magazine*), and *Utah Holiday* magazine have also made lasting contributions to the form. *BYU Studies* published Leonard Arrington's charming autobiographical essay.[8] One of the glories of *Exponent II* is its small personal accounts of individual lives that might not otherwise see the light of day, particularly the problems of housewifery that loom so large in a woman's life but are all too easy to dismiss as "unimportant." Helen Candland Stark laments, "Since I was the eldest of nine children, with no sisters until after four brothers, I naturally fell into the role of Mama's little helper. In addition, Mama had a legitimate escape hatch—she liked to work in the garden. So I manned, or rather, womanned the kitchen. . . . Was there no end except bed? Something in me cried for some time of my own."[9] Ardith N. Walker asks, "What's a Mother to Do?"

> I've been jogging every morning for ten months, three weeks, and two days. I've had to fight off mad dogs, ignore jeering high school students, brave blinding snow storms, endure twelve degree weather. I've tripped through ankle-deep chuck holes, inhaled stunning odors on garbage days, and worst of all had to slog uphill the last half of the way . . . but I was convinced it was worth it. . . . Then yesterday an orthopedic surgeon told my husband there is nothing worse on feet and knees than jogging.[10]

Emma Lou Thayne's personal tribute to tennis is more upbeat. She describes the thrill of playing in a tournament during which the adult she is merges with the girl she was. "It may stay as one of the real recognitions that only now and then is it allowed us—to see the gratuities of eternity—that growing older is the richest kind of blending, for it multiplies as it combines. On the court, in the heart, in the plan, the growing not old, but older is probably the only way of knowing how much right there is in the journey."[11]

*BYU Today,* one of the best alumni newspapers, is fortunate in having some fine essayists on the BYU campus. Laura Wadley, at the time assistant editor of *BYU Studies,* contributes to the nostalgic, occasional form. She makes lists that stay in the mind. In the school's centennial commemoration, she recounts its blessings:

> The short shaky climb up the stepladder to the telescope to see the moon suddenly spring close. . . . The lazy lighthearted sunny afternoon class in Mark Twain in which the teacher can say Pap Finn was a real Adult Aaronic and be perfectly understood. . . . Brigham Young standing silent at the upper edge of the campus. . . . The long rows of beguilingly bound books, of test tubes, or sewing machines, typewriters, lathes, paintings and clay pots. The life of the mind, the skill of the hands, all that will take us from where we are to where we most earnestly desire to be . . . and finally . . . one man coming to the Center of the darkness of the deep of the Marriott Center, the light gathering around him as he walks. He begins: "My beloved brothers and sisters. . . .

Clifton Jolley's confessionals also appear in *BYU Today.* He recounts his trips abroad, his former deceptions as an undergraduate, and, most delightfully, his opinions as a father. In "Food Is Important, But . . ." he claims to be profoundly concerned about pollution and the rapidly diminishing food supply. But he has a problem—actually, five problems: three girls and two boys.

> You see, I am not particularly fond of children. As a matter of fact I am almost certain to loathe your children—wretched little creatures who are more likely to wipe their noses on my trousers' leg than thrill me with their sweetness. So if you were to suggest that you were planning to limit your family to one or two children, I would probably be enthusiastic. If, on the other hand you were to suggest that I limit the number of my children well . . . that's my problem.

He claims his own children as gifts, and his wife agrees:

You see the last baby was absolutely perfect. . . . Oh, I know it's hor-
rifying. The idea even horrifies me a little—all those orchards filling up.
Los Angeles getting no nicer. But then again, there is Sarah. She'll eat
rocks, and anyone who'll eat rocks can't be too much of a threat to the
environment.[13]

*Utah Holiday*, which ceased publishing in 1993, made a strong contribution to the art of the comic essay, and its classic is "I Remember Ernie," by Jaron Summers, former BYU student newspaper editor. His portrait of the late Ernest Wilkinson is funny, and it will awaken memories
in anyone who ever had his hand crunched by "Ernie." But it manages,
too, to bring a lump to the throat, as the best comedy can do. Having
described Ernie as a "Tasmanian Devil . . . a giant badger . . . a troll,"
Jaron elaborates on Wilkinson's "compulsion to prove to BYU and the
rest of the world that he was as stout as Jimmy Cagney and as rugged as
John Wayne." He did this through his handshake: "He was proud how
he could outcrunch thousands of the frosh and just to make sure no one
forgot what he was doing, Ernie had someone standing by with a pocket
counter." Years later, Summers writes, he returned to Utah where he saw
Ernie coming toward him: He had been sick, and had lost weight; he
looked weak. "Time had won." Jaron is touched as he takes "Wilkinson's
hand softly in mine," only to be attacked again by the iron grip:

> Instantly the fire blazed in his eyes. He clamped down on my five
> unsuspecting fingers; and I knew what it would be like to have my hand
> tangled in an electric flour mill. He gritted his teeth and chortled. . . .
>
> And then he let up, and that awful pressure faded and he shuffled
> down the corridor to his meeting; and I think if I hadn't loved the old
> bugger so much I would have body-checked him through the nearest
> window, or tried to.[14]

## II

As an undergraduate at the University of Utah, I amused myself
by writing feature articles for the *Utah Chronicle*. They covered such
important topics as my phobias, advice on dating, and pseudo surveys.
One day, the father of one of my good friends, a writer on the *Salt Lake
Tribune*, called me into his office. He had been reading my pieces and
he wanted to offer a bit of useful advice from an old pro. It was "Never

use the first person pronoun." My work was studded with "I's"! Why, there were three or four of them in one paragraph. Such egomania had no place in serious journalism.

I have never forgotten his advice, and I have seldom obeyed it.

I am happy that the writers of the Mormon essay do not obey it either. I maintain that the "I's" are what distinguish the personal essay from other forms of literature and that all the best ones combine the best use of three "I's" ("I's," eyes, ayes). Like any other pat structural analysis, this can be carried too far, but I like it because it allows me to discuss my personal favorites.

At first glance it seems that women writers use more first person pronouns than other writers do, but I have not documented this. I notice that my favorite among my own attempts, "Mr. Mustard Plaster," has seven "I's" in the first paragraph and that "Counseling the Brethren," by Laurel Thatcher Ulrich, has three "I's" and several "me's":

> The scent of shaving lotion startled me. It was like finding a "No Trespassing" sign in some familiar patch of woods. I'd walked through that door a hundred times, would teach Sunday School in the same classroom an hour later, yet the spice in the air made me an adventuress.
>
> "Hey, Sister Ulrich, this is a priesthood meeting," an elder teased from the end of the row as I sat down. His good humor made me feel more comfortable, but less exotic. He knew I'd been invited.[15]

Using so many "I's" could mean an overpowering ego at work, or it could represent a refreshing willingness to share oneself. I submit that it is less egotistical in the traditional sense of the word to use the simple I than to assume a royal we. The I takes complete responsibility, for its own failings and peccadillos—a nice change from the monumental I, style of many sermons and articles in our past and present. Nor are these "I's" afraid to make grandiose claims for themselves. Gene England, in what he tells me is his own favorite, begins this way:

> The first time I participated in the "Hosanna Shout" I felt the presence of actual beings from another world joining us in that cry of praise and the following "Hosanna Anthem." That was in the Celestial Room of the Oakland Temple in 1964, following President David O. McKay's dedicatory prayer—And I do believe, strange as it perhaps seems for me—a skeptical, rationalistic, university—trained professor of English—

to be saying this, that we were joined by spiritual beings—whether former prophets, angelic messengers or repentant sinners—who had similar reasons to our own to rejoice.[16]

His description of the dedication of the Washington, D.C. temple is in a personal style—some might claim too personal for publication, dropping names of good friends, almost as in a letter home.

*Exponent II*'s editors have claimed that the non-threatening "throwaway" quality of their paper was meant to encourage women to emerge from their cocoons and, if not to fly away, at least to test their wings. Although I sometimes worry that the throw-away paper lacks the permanence researchers and future readers need, I continue to appreciate the diverse voices published there. Its coverage of the International Women's Year conferences in various states illustrates the variety of "I's" attending. Rebecca Cornwall cries out: "I am not comforted by the reality that Mormon women were misinformed and manipulated by radical conservatives . . . I am disturbed that Mormon women were so easily manipulated."[17] While Belva Ashton says, "As I read some of the negative news reports of the Utah IWY Conference, I could not believe they were reporting the same conference I was attending. I felt in general that it was great."[18] "Gospel principles unify us, but the application of those principles should help us be ourselves—developing in unique directions suited to our unique purposes in contributing to the kingdom," says Diane McKinney,[19] and the personal essays throughout *Exponent II* show how the process works.

The eye is the ability of the writers to see more clearly than ordinary folk, to record what is seen in selective detail and to shape the record to support the other "I's."

Edward Geary's eye is not bloodshot, though it occasionally holds a tear. Like a camera it records and preserves artifacts of our culture. The eye of his essays is truly conservative, conserving and generously preserving humor, characters, and scenes from the past. "Goodbye to Poplarhaven" is the Geary eye at its clearest: "The town of my childhood, Huntington, Utah, is no older than my grandparents and contains nothing that is likely to outlast my grandchildren; yet from it has come whatever sense I have of human continuity." He compares the town to the Lombardy poplar tree, which is "not a long-lived tree; its limbs are brittle and its soft wood subject to decay. This pattern of early growth and early decline held true for the town as well as its trees." His brief history of the town is wistful but realistic: "It was into this gradual and gentle decay that I was born, and I grew up in an old town. The people were old because the majority of each new generation left the valley and only a few, like my parents, remained out of nostalgia or hope, to have in their turn children who would grow up to move away."[20]

In "Disorder and Early Joy," the reader shares Geary's finely tuned sense of humor as the eye sees that "to grow up in rural Utah is to inherit a tradition of unpainted outbuildings, tumbled-down fences and superannuated farm implements; a world held together by baling-wire." He quotes a friend who maintains that a "true Utahn cannot be perfectly happy unless he has an old Buick rusting away in the pasture," or, from Geary's childhood, "an old Dodge with wooden spoked wheels, decaying gently under an apricot tree beside my grandfather's tool shed."[21]

Samuel Taylor and Wayne Carver are also able to transform their past with the magic wand of the fiction-writer, often using their gifts to turn essay into memoir. Carver's "A Child's Christmas in Utah," a Mormon version of the famous Dylan Thomas story, beautifully recreates the rural atmosphere of a Utah that is past.[22] Taylor's "The Second Coming of Santa Claus: Christmas in a Polygamous Family" is only one of a whole collection of witty essays in which Taylor evokes a particular time and place in Mormon life.[23] His voice is always true to the form, a voice easily recognizable, often endearing, a voice that truly speaks for his selective eye.

The eye of the Mormon essayist is nearly always looking upon the past, applying it to the present with sadness, yet with hope. Even in "Death of a Child," the unsentimental account of an unbearable experience, we are reminded that hopelessness is brief and does not endure.

> Late that afternoon . . . he died. His spirit struggled to free itself from that wasted body, and he was gone.
> Oh, how empty was that room. I wrapped what was left of his little body tenderly in a blanket and held it close in my rocking chair as I had yearned so long to do. He could feel the pain no longer. And when at last I gave him up to the mortician, he received the body with tears on his cheeks.

That body had grown in four months from a child to a wasted old man. And his spirit had grown large enough to fill all of our hearts and lives with faith and expectation until we meet again.[24]

If tragedy can be described as ending, as permanent loss, then tragedy is foreign to most Mormon writers. As Maureen Ursenbach Beecher has put it, "Even in applying martyrdom to the murder of Joseph Smith is found the doctrinal assurance that his death was not a tragic end to this life but a glorious promise for the next."[25]

Many aye-saying essays are written testimonies. Gene England bears his testimony when he describes the emotional significance of the temple, as he lays his hands in blessing on his car, or when he launches a new publication. In fact, most of the essayists I have mentioned bear their testimonies to life itself, its variety, its humor, its pain, and to the many lessons it teaches.

Lowell Bennion's personal essays are not life transformed into art, or life transformed by art, as in the works of Jolley and Taylor; they are bits and pieces of himself, collected and presented for inspection. It can almost be said that his life and his work are one, all of a piece created out of whole cloth. "Brother Bennion" has dedicated his professional and religious life to "carrying water on both shoulders," that is, to helping the student to reconcile the two worlds of university and church, the life of the mind and the life of the spirit. Bennion's students will recognize the voice in this paragraph:

> I look upon religion and secular thought as being complementary . . .
> as well as conflicting. . . . I no longer seek to harmonize them . . . in the
> sense of expecting them to give me identical views of reality (as I once did).
> I reject, for example, those well meant efforts of people whom I respect,
> who try to make a biology or geology text out of Genesis . . . or who read a
> theory of physics into D&C 93. For me, the scriptures declare the existence
> of God and his will and man's obligation to God and fellow-man, and they
> leave me free to explore nature and human nature as I will.[26]

Typically, Bennion declares the inalienable right to free agency in all of his works but accompanies it with a plea for humility. I have heard him say often, "Our religion is bigger than any one man's conception of it."

Perhaps the best part of the aye-saying essay is its humor. Mormons, usually a jolly people, often seem afraid of humor in print. We may need to be reminded that in the personal essay the writers speak only for themselves, not for anyone else, certainly not for God. They are therefore free to laugh at themselves. And if they find no one else is laughing, that is the chance they must take.

Most Mormon humor is gentle. It may be applied to institutions, but it is usually pointed inward. I think of Jolley's descriptions of his children, Taylor's accounts of polygamous family life, and Geary's regional portraits, like this brief one of Bert Westover "who reputedly had fought at San Juan Hill with Teddy Roosevelt. . . . Except for his own funeral, I don't ever remember seeing him inside the church house. However, he used to declare his intentions of moving away somewhere before the Millennium because his house would be the first place they hit coming over the hill from the cemetery and they'd eat him out of house and home."[27]

Certain characteristic themes recur throughout all the personal essays: the loss of old buildings and old towns; the difficulty of living one's religion creatively; the search for authenticity and wholeness; the need to mend fences, to preserve eccentricity. And through them all, there is the desire to reach out without striking out, a striving for the right word, the delicate balance.

## Notes

1. Richard H. Cracroft and Neal E. Lambert, eds., section introduction to *A Believing People: Literature of the Latter-day Saints* (Provo, Utah: Brigham Young University Press, 1974), 201.

2. Frances Lee Menlove, "The Challenge of Honesty," *Dialogue: A Journal of Mormon Thought* 1 (Spring 1966): 45–53.

3. Karl Keller, "Every Soul Has Its South," *Dialogue: A Journal of Mormon Thought* 1 (Summer 1966): 72–79.

4. Carlos S. Whiting, "An Honorable Surrender: The Experience of Conversion," *Dialogue: A Journal of Mormon Thought* 2 (Spring 1967): 40–47.

5. Carole C. Hansen, "Death of a Son," *Dialogue: A Journal of Mormon Thought* 2 (Autumn 1967): 91–96.

6. Victor Cline, "The Faith of a Psychologist: A Personal Document," *Dialogue: A Journal of Mormon Thought* 1 (Spring 1966): 54–67; Lowell L. Bennion, "For by Grace Are Ye Saved," *Dialogue: A Journal of Mormon Thought* 1 (Winter 1966): 100–104; Edward A. Geary, "Goodbye to Poplarhaven," *Dialogue: A Journal of Mormon Thought* 8 (Summer 1972): 56–82.

7. Jaroldeen Asplund Edwards, "Full House," *Dialogue: A Journal of Mormon Thought* 6 (Summer 1971): 9–16.

8. Leonard J. Arrington, "The Historian as Entrepreneur: A Personal Essay," *BYU Studies* 17 (Winter 1977): 193–209.

9. Helen Candland Stark, "The Good Woman Syndrome, or When Is Enough, Enough?" *Exponent II* 3 (1976): 16.

10. Ardith N. Walker, "What's a Mother to Do?" *Exponent II* 5 (1976): 16.

11. Emma Lou Thayne, "The Getting There," *Exponent II* 4 (1977): 11.

12. Laura Wadley, "The Moon Spring Close: Shadows and Foreshadows," *BYU Today* 30 (May 1976): 9.

13. Clifton Holt Jolley, "Food Is Important, But . . . ," *BYU Today* 31 (Apr. 1977): 23.

14. Jaron Sommers, "I Remember Ernie: The Wilkinson Generation," *Utah Holiday* 5 (3 Dec. 1975): 15–16.

15. Laurel Thatcher Ulrich, "Counseling the Brethren," *Dialogue: A Journal of Mormon Thought* 9 (Summer 1974): 68–70.

16. Eugene England, "The Hosanna Shout in Washington, D.C.," *Dialogue: A Journal of Mormon Thought* 11 (Summer 1974): 62–67.

17. Rebecca Cornwall, "Mormon Denial," *Exponent II* 4 (1977): 5.

18. Belva Ashton, "Magnificent Women," *Exponent II* 4 (1977): 5.

19. Diane McKinney (Kellogg), "Dividends of Diversity," *Exponent II* 5 (Winter 1979): 2.

20. Geary, "Goodbye to Poplarhaven," 56–58.

21. Edward A. Geary, "Disorder and Early Joy," *Dialogue: A Journal of Mormon Thought* 9 (Fall 1974): 61.

22. Wayne Carver, "A Child's Christmas in Utah," *Dialogue: A Journal of Mormon Thought* 7 (Autumn 1972): 11–16.

23. Samuel W. Taylor, "The Second Coming of Santa Claus: Christmas in a Polygamous Family," *Dialogue: A Journal of Mormon Thought* 7 (Autumn 1972): 7–11.

24. Hansen, "Death of a Son," 95–96.

25. Maureen Ursenbach Beecher, "A Thread of Tragedy—But Not the Whole Cloth," *Journal of Mormon History* 3 (1976): 106.

26. Lowell L. Bennion, "Carrying Water on Both Shoulders," *Dialogue: A Journal of Mormon Thought* 6 (Spring 1971): 112.

27. Geary, "Goodbye to Poplarhaven," 244.

# I
# LEAVING HOME

# YESTERDAY
# THE WARDHOUSE

When I was a girl, our wardhouse appeared in booklets showing some architectural oddities of Salt Lake City. We were proud that it looked so little like a church. It was squat and white with a round, towerlike appurtenance on the front. It was once mistaken for a dairy, and I think now it may have been a true community center.

There was always a wedding reception, and I was always a bridesmaid. I was always appearing in some play or other, or serving at a dinner, or waiting around hoping (or fearing) to be danced with. I recited scriptures of my own choosing, by heart, every Sunday morning for three months straight-running. Standing just in front of the choir seats, I recited "The Waltz" by Dorothy Parker. I sang "Elijah" with a crowd of other monotones at stake conference. I was thrilled one day when David O. McKay himself put his arm around me as he stood in a silver tie that matched his hair. I won first place in "Untrained Scripture Readings" at the speech festival. I wore a drop-shoulder dress in the roadshow. As secretary of the Sunday School, I sat in front of the whole congregation, taking illegible notes and caring for my little sister, who always sat beside me. Once I wound a maypole in a queen contest. At the end of one lucky streamer was a box holding the crown. I didn't win the crown, but I did learn to waltz.

I recall that ward carnivals, held outdoors on the parking lot, were gambling affairs. We pitched pennies and paid to vote for royalty. In fast and testimony meeting, I stood and thanked God for saving my mother's life in direct answer to my prayers. The bishops in those days were always uncles or cousins of mine and suitably benign and distant.

My fantasy life was bounded by the "ward show." In our neighbor-hood I collected for the budget. Each contribution entitled a family to a white card for free movies on Friday and Saturday nights. I myself always arrived a half-hour early and saved the front row. If the show was especially good, I saw it both nights. High up in the back of the amusement hall (as it was unashamedly called in those days) were three little holes above a painted, built-in ladder. I envied the projectionist who climbed that ladder every weekend and disappeared through a ridiculously small trap door.

Although the ward shows were family outings, they were not fam-ily movies, but horrendous affairs which scared me for years. I don't recall seeing those characters so appreciated today—Laurel and Hardy, W. C. Fields, Charlie Chaplain—but if Louis Hayward, Robert Donat, and Tyrone Power ever come in again, I will welcome them back. How I ached for Louis Hayward, whose beautiful face was shut up in that terrible iron mask simply because his nefarious brother (also played by Louis Hayward) had tricked him. I cried my own canal over the sufferings of Power as he built the Suez Canal, despite the death of his faithful Annabella. My throat choked up over *Beau Geste* and *The Four Feathers,* which somehow run together in my mind as a double bill. My loyalties seemed equally divided between the prisons of France and the sands of Arabia. And nobody ever thought to tell me that the sufferings of the Count of Monte Cristo would disturb my dreams. I remember walking home after the ward shows, watching the shadows, listening for stealthy footsteps, running the last cowardly steps to my door.

Primary was primarily arts and crafts and singing. After school I always stopped in at home, cut a lemon, divided it with a cousin, and strolled on to Primary where we sucked the lemons and flipped the seeds under the benches. One day when our teacher, for some obscure reason, asked us to make faces, we just took an extra slurp.

We were Larks and Bluebirds and Seagulls, which names seem to me less dated and more soaring than Top Pilots and CTR Pilots. I learned to bake bread, to embroider (I put a lily on my dishtowel), and to babysit (at twenty-five cents for the evening). I don't recall the lesson material ex-cept as it touched on the Lost Tribes. We decided they were on the North Star. Given today's urban blight, I think that a felicitous idea.

MIA (now Young Men and Young Women) seemed mainly social. I'm sure we had lessons there too, but the only one I remember was given by a young woman who later had nine children. She told us it was better to be born poor than not be born at all.

Arriving early has always been one of my vices. Often I arrived early at MIA, where I would perch on a step reading a nitty-gritty tome by Joseph Fielding Smith or Oscar McConkie. One of the boys in the ward, an older and wiser man of fifteen, grew alarmed at my fanaticism. One day he presented me with his personal copies of *Lad, A Dog* and *Thirty Seconds over Tokyo*. I read them dutifully, never thinking to ask why he hadn't chosen something racier if he was that concerned over my potential spinsterhood.

Some of us met at MIA in order to ride to the Tabernacle where we sang in the All-Church Music Festival. As we waited, we danced in the streets, while some turned cartwheels and bayed at the sky. When I was finally allowed to date, I dated boys in the ward. When one of them left for his mission, I gave a memorized scripture. I remember that I transposed parts of it, telling the audience quite sincerely that "as the spirit without the body is dead, so are works without faith."

It seems to me that the wardhouse saw me lovingly into womanhood, turning me graciously over to the LDS Institute of Religion at the University of Utah. The wardhouse today is treated with more respect, beginning with its name. We call it The Church, and we are warned to keep our kids from tearing the phone off the walls. My children sit with folded arms learning "reverence." I don't recall hearing much about reverence in our wardhouse, but I think I felt it, even while the little ones munched goodies in the aisles during sacrament meeting. Nowadays, after sacrament meeting, we march out, row by row, with an usher to guide our steps. The foyer is always jammed with members loath to leave until the strain of being reverent has worn off.

The amusement hall (see recreation) is now the Cultural Hall. We have "programs" there, candlelight dinners, and arts festivals. One year the Primary children gave the Christmas program instead of the teachers, and it showed considerable polish. We had a ward show once, and I sat on the front row just for old times' sake. The panavision nearly ruined my eyes, and our children found the Brothers Grimm pretty grim.

The doors to our church are usually locked against the marauding hordes, and, of course, my children can't walk there. I must deliver them and then hover about waiting to sweep down and rescue them from the dangers of the dark parking lot and swerving street. The urge to run through the cultural hall is as strong as ever and sometimes spills over into the chapel, which is separated by a folding door. My wardhouse was mine, as much a part of me as my home and family, and I gave it as little thought when I was young. The joy and comradeship I felt there is still with me. Yet, especially today, it seems the nuclear family must build a nuclear shelter out of home evenings and family outings. What will my children remember with nostalgia? A day in Amish country where bearded gentlemen ride by in closed carriages, laughing, always laughing, while buses and cars snort behind them, unable to pass. A weekend in New York City where a man rushes two blocks through the Christmas rush to catch a bus because an elderly lady left her purse. They may remember waking up in Williamsburg to find a light snow all over the yule log and fresh greens in all the windows. A boat ride to Nantucket where seagulls greeted us. And a day in Nauvoo where they were less impressed with Joseph Smith's house than with the noble expanse of river and real wheat growing in the fields.

One Sunday our entire sacrament meeting program was presented by the youth: youth bishopric, youth speakers, youth musicians. One of the speakers, a fluent, golden-haired lad of seventeen, described the world as, he said, Satan would have it: a world in which white and black hate each other, a world which fights senseless wars for obscure reasons, and a world which persecutes people for the length of their hair. I was struck by this thought: Those of us who grew up in my old wardhouse were seldom concerned with such matters. We were part of the Silent Generation. And then another thought: Though we were quite provincial, we had not been crippled by a world war or by the Depression. We were allowed to grow in peace. Because our parents had been leveled by the Depression, the members of our ward were also economically equal. Can the security we felt in the old wardhouse be transferred to the church family of today?

I would like to design a church building that brings us together again. It would be round and surrounded by trees or mountains, prairie or desert. It would be made of the materials of this earth. Its doors would stand open to visitors, its windows open to light. Its round, soundproof foyer would be large enough that Mormons might greet each other—as they must—but without chairs, lest they linger too long. The cultural hall would be suitably separate from the chapel, and the chapel would be semi-circular because I love to look into the faces of my brothers and sisters. Our leaders would not sit over us, but with us. The classrooms would be semi-circular too, warmly painted and carpeted for comfort and communication.

Yes, our building would accommodate the innocence and the diversity of today's church and still reflect the joy and laughter, the worship and reverence that have always been part of our religion and part of us.

[1970]

# MR. MUSTARD PLASTER

I never intended to leave Utah. In fact I didn't leave until I was sixteen, and that was only on a trip to my father's hometown in Wyoming. I didn't make it to California until I was twenty and had only one requirement in a mate: that he never want to leave Utah either. Three months after my marriage found me going to Washington, D.C. on the arm of a rising young legislative assistant. Since then I have left Utah many times, always thinking I am finally weaned away.

The first time, however, my mother thought I was going to the hinterlands. She didn't say much when we drove off, but a couple of weeks later the desk attendant at our apartment delivered an urgent special-delivery package: a bottle of high potency vitamins, which Mother was sure we would need to cope with the wickedness of the nation's capital. She was expressing a distrust of Washington that Utahns have shared ever since Johnston's War. Whenever we return to Utah, we find ourselves assuring people that no, the black residents of Resurrection City did not ruin the Reflecting Pool so that it had to be drained and paved over; and that no, the Lincoln Monument has not sunk into the Potomac (yet). We tell them that we survived the peace marches and the burning of Fourteenth Street the same way they did, by crouching in front of the television set. They are surprised to hear that we have never met the president or been mugged in front of our house (though other Mormons have, of course).

We counter their questions by asking why Salt Lakers are so eager to ape the problems of the Big Cities by building skyscrapers to block out the temple and freeways to create slums. I always soft-pedal the fear I have felt in Washington, especially the chill of driving down Constitution Avenue the day after the Fourteenth Street riots when it was lined with rows and rows of soldiers with bayonets. When asked about peace marches, we tell how my husband, when blocked at the bridge, innocently rolled down his window so the marchers could dance to the strains of the Tab Choir on his stereo tape.

Even though I feign sophistication when talking with the home-town folks, I am convinced that they who leave Utah, no matter how mature they think themselves, do so with a mixture of innocence, fear, and self-confidence that brings to mind the old saying, "You can take the girl out of Utah, but you can't take Utah out of the girl."

We settled first in a highrise on the Virginia side of the Potomac. We could not quite see the spires of Georgetown University on the left; on the right we could not quite see the Iwo Jima Monument. We did have a clear view of our neighbor's living room. The things that disturbed me most about apartment living were the necessity of having to chat through chains on the neighbors' doors and learning that people did not leap to join the church because I refused their coffee.

But Washington is a lovely city, and I decided to apply for work at the loveliest building, the National Gallery of Art. When they asked me how many hours of art history I had taken, I moved up the Mall to the Library of Congress where I got on as a clerk-typist GS-4. My superiors were a bit apologetic about my M.A. in English, but I assured them I was happy with my appointment to that old ship, green then, covered with barnacles and protected by Neptune and his lusty nymphs. The secret warrens of this grand old building, unknown to the casual visitor, seemed peaceful, but who knew what explosives lined its shelves? I loved to look up at the great dome, to study the paintings in the panels, to walk slowly down the arching marble staircase. I loved the marble restrooms with their giant fixtures that made even the private business of the body seem dignified.

I was in the American Law Division of the Congressional Reference Section, where my typewriter, crammed between rows of law books, was set before a window miraculously framing the Supreme Court Building. I had morning sickness then and was constantly burrowing into my soda crackers, chewing as I typed. For relief I would go out and lie down on a bench behind one of the display cases or repair to the restroom to retch silently. The library hid me and guarded me. My superiors were always understanding, but one day when I returned from sick leave (again), the second-in-command called me to his private office. "Oh, oh," I thought, "this is the sack at last." But he smiled sympathetically. "Got the morning sickness, eh? Well, keep the tummy full!" Whereupon he gave me an assignment he said was more in keeping with my training—research in the main reading room.

A cohort of mine from Utah worked next door as a secretary to foreign lawyers who were dealing in exciting stuff behind the Iron Curtain. These men were all exotic and older. Whenever I passed by, they made what I was sure were ribald remarks in Romanian. One day my friend and I were on the elevator with one of these lawyers, who looked pitifully elderly and broken to my eye, and coughed consumptively, complaining that he couldn't seem to clear up his chest condition. Said I jocularly, "What you need is an old-fashioned mustard plaster."

"What's that?"

I explained that it was an old Utah remedy.

"Why not show me?" he said, and since he lived in the same apartment complex, I agreed to come over with a mustard plaster.

It was a mark of our innocence that my husband did not even ask where I was going as I departed the apartment at ten o'clock that night. Carrying my supplies, I took the elevator to the tenth floor in the adjoining building. The lawyer opened the door, bowed elegantly in his pajamas, and locked the door behind me. I found myself in an apartment like ours except that he could see the Washington Monument. He clicked off the lights that I might have a better view and, before I could mix up my mustard, had encircled me in his skinny arms and grazed my cheek with a kiss.

I dropped my supplies and leaped backward. He was in no condition to engage me if I were unwilling, and I spoke sharply: "Get over on that bed and lie down. I came here to put a mustard plaster on you, and I'm going to do it." He lay back wordlessly, baring his concave chest, while I quickly spread the dull-yellow stuff over a cloth I had cut in the shape of a vest. I slapped the cloth on his chest, covered it with another, insulated the whole mess with a large piece of brown paper, and rebuttoned his pajama top. Without further instructions, I made for the door.

He stopped me as I was leaving. Holding his plaster close, he jerked a yellow rose from a vase on a table and thrust it at me. "Please accept this," he said, coughing. "I have never met a woman like you in my whole life."

He fell back on his bed, and I let myself out, rose in hand. (What burning passions did he feel for me afterward?)

Hadn't anyone ever told me that young women, even married ones, do not visit bachelors, even elderly ones, in their apartments at night, and that elderly bachelors do not usually have mustard plasters on their minds?

Years later in a brief reunion with the friend who had worked with the lawyers, she told me of her encounter with Mr. Mustard Plaster. A single girl at the time, she had taken a drive with him one Sunday afternoon. Afterward he had invited her to his apartment to share the view. She had leapt out of his embrace with the words, "Please, I'm a Mormon!" and had added, "Besides, this is Sunday!" His laughter haunts her yet, along with the nickname he gave her, "The Never on Sunday Girl."

[1971]

# AN ART DECO CHILDHOOD

While reading an article about 1930s and 1940s furniture called "Deco Echoes," I heard echoes of my own—voices from the furniture friends of my childhood, and I asked myself, "Where have all those cherished pieces gone?"

What, for instance, has happened to the blue mirrored coffee table that occupied a place of honor in the living room of my tender years? It was undoubtedly the same blue mirror that graced the New York restaurants of the 1930s. The table was a good place to sail little dream ships full of hopes about the stories I was forever mailing off to eastern publishers only to receive polite rejection slips written as if the editors had not guessed I was only twelve years old.

When I grew older, I searched for signs of movie star beauty in the blue face reflected in its glass top. As a little girl, I had been favorably compared to Shirley Temple. Would I grow up to become Lana Turner?

Where is the intricately stenciled cedar chest my mother gave me to store my Scarlett O'Hara doll and her wardrobe? The yellow lid of the small chest was the setting for an elaborate wedding between Scarlett and a wooden doll named Pinocchio, which belonged to my brother Tom. Tom loved dolls but felt that a storybook character was the only one he could own without being labeled sissy. This wedding was only one event in my lifetime infatuation with *Gone with the Wind*. I read the book under the covers with a flashlight when I was ten. It was instructive. Not only did it provide worthy insights into the Southern mind and the antebellum period in American history, but it answered my most burning question about babies. When Rhett Butler carried Scarlett up the stairs, the result was little Bonnie Blue.

The bed of my childhood was art deco, too. I used its high brown metal foot and headboards to scare myself. How could such a bed scare a child? The lights from the living room, sneaking in through a crack under my bedroom door, splayed out over the ridged metal and conjured visions of hellfire. Even though my Mormon upbringing told me that hell was mostly my own shortcomings, I envisioned snakes and dragons gleaned from my wider reading in scary stories. I loved being scared, but my brother didn't. Sleeping in the same room with me, he would rush out screaming at my eloquent visions. My parents, thinking that he was trying to trick them into letting him stay up, were vexed. He never told on me, though. I could be vicious when ratted on.

A recent visit to the family homestead revealed another old friend rotting away in the orchard—none other than the wooden, brass-trimmed ice box, the very kind people are polishing and selling for horrendous sums in antique shops today.

My father looked askance at anybody who would think such a creature worth saving. It was a great day for him when he could trade his weekly trips to the ice house for a new refrigerator. But he didn't tealize how much I enjoyed shivering with him as he carried out the large mirrored block almost as blue as our table, wrapped it carefully in burlap, and tucked it gently into the trunk of Lizzie, our '28 Chevy. On those trips my father could usually be persuaded to stop at Laura Larson's for some green-pineapple ice cream. Laura Larson's was the only store in Salt Lake to make the mellow treat that was almost the death of my little brother Dennis. Driving with one hand and holding the cones with the other, Dad failed to notice that the door on my side of the car was ajar. Dennis rolled off my lap out onto the street, and the green-pineapple rolled onto me. Fortunately, Dennis lived—along with my guilty memory of the ice cream, ice house gang.

Good old Lizzie! A gray-green box on wheels, she was graced with a silver radiator cap with wings like a ship's figurehead. For years Dad was forced to start her by cranking. He accomplished this by inserting a metal rod into the starter shaft while keeping one foot on the running board and leaping lithely into the seat and hitting the starter pedal before the engine sputtered out. This was the car that won my mother. He bought it just before their engagement.

When our family was finally blessed with a little sister, we prevailed upon Dad to rig up the trunk so that two of the children could lie down in it with a blanket, a pillow, and some lunch on our way to

Ephraim, a small town in central Utah, home of some of Dad's relatives—the longest trip Lizzie ever took.

After we grew up and left home, my father propped Lizzie up on some wooden blocks in the orchard, and, after we got used to visiting her there in her dignified old age, he sold her to a teenage boy for sixty dollars. It saddened me to see that this boy had no trouble driving away in the art deco carriage of my childhood.

Our wood stove in the center of the living room, its pipe reaching through the ceiling, was a reminder of my bouts with "la grippe" which became in our family lexicon, "The Grip," named thus because of its grip on my throat—a steamy hand clutching my vocal chords. My father and mother had three treatments for The Grip: heat towels on the stove and slip them on my chest just before they burst into flame; heat bricks and place them at my feet in bed; wrap ice-cold cloths around my neck and insulate them with a hot towel. These comforting rituals measured out the winters of my secure childhood.

And where is the square ebony table with carved legs that used to stand imposingly before the living room window? It doubled as a dining room table when company came, but during the week, I composed some fine works on that table in the middle of family home evening which in those days was every night. Some of these were homework assignments, but others were "written testimonies," assigned by a certain Mr. Romstoff, who, according to his thrilling sacrament meeting accounts, had survived a hair-raising escape from Russia. A "White Russian," he had met Tolstoy and was now living quietly with a housekeeper not far from our house.

Noticing my perch at the black table, Mr. Romstoff suggested that if I were as diligent a writer as I appeared, he could probably place some of my work in *The Improvement Era*. With the money, I could buy a typewriter to replace the one I was borrowing.

So each week for six weeks, he assigned me a subject: temple marriage, college plans, and other goals a teenage Mormon girl could aspire to. He even talked of laminating my little testimonies for possible missionary cards! This was heady stuff, and it kept me churning out compositions at a spectacular rate despite my father's skeptical, "I don't think Mr. Romstoff is ever going to get you a typewriter!"

One day strange news was revealed through whispers in our ward. Mr. Romstoff had been found out! The Man Who Knew Tolstoy was living in sin with his housekeeper, a fact that threw doubt on his tales of intrigue about the Russian Revolution.

My mother sold the remodeled player piano of my youth. It withstood my third grade version of "Ah, Sweet Mystery of Life," a song I inflicted on ward members during the only recital of my life. I loved the song because it was the theme of a glorious movie starring Nelson Eddy and Jeanette MacDonald, my favorite singers. Today, as I watch my teenage son painstakingly typing out the words—or grunts—to the pop music of such incomprehensible groups as "Kool and the Gang," I can't help but feel culturally superior. Surely the music of my art deco childhood was on a higher intellectual level. I still remember some of the words: "When I'm calling you . . . oo . . . oo . . . ooo . . . oo . . . oo. . . ."

[1981]

# GIRL OF THE LIMBERLOST
# AND LONESOME PINE

My childhood summers were dreams dreamed out of books, long walks, and cherry tree climbs. Once a week I would set out, books under my arm, for the library where I would lose myself in its cool stacks. Then I would trudge back home to arrange myself halfway up in the cherry tree whose limbs had conveniently formed a perfect chair. Or I would lie on a blanket on the side lawn until spotted by one of the neighborhood gang and talked into a game of baseball or a trip to the candy store.

I can remember more about books than about actual events in my peaceful life. *Girl of the Limberlost or Lonesome Pine,* I was, Nancy Drew, Tarzana of the Apes. The books I read then were not what we now call children's classics. Certainly I read *Jane Eyre* and *Wuthering Heights* for the wrong reasons. I missed the clear feminist message in the former, retaining only its romanticism, and thought the latter unnecessarily brutal. I read *Madame Bovary,* too, but I was much older before its meaning dawned on me. After I was grown, my mother confessed that she had deliberately planted certain "facts of life" books within reach so that I would ask her the right questions. I never did.

I loved *Little Women* so much that I organized a summer theater production of my own three-act version. The backyard was transformed into a stage with a bedspread draped as a curtain over the clothesline. I played Jo, of course, even though I was deeply disappointed in her for failing to marry Laurie.

I received a new book every Christmas. I say new, even though it was probably a bequest from my grandmother's or my mother's library. Through *Alice in Wonderland, The Little Princess,* and *The Secret Garden,* I came to feel like a transplanted being. England was my true home, I felt. I had been dropped on Utah through some cosmic mistake. I was comforted, though, by sleeping outside in our backyard where I looked at the stars and wondered about the world beyond my private mountain. It stood next to Mount Olympus but was not nearly as formidable and was named by my girlfriend and me—"Mount Longhollow."

Summers were gestation periods that allowed my seeking soul to wander in vacant fields, to wade through ditches and morning glories, only occasionally forced to come home to help with the dishes or the other children. It was a time for renewal, for reading the books I wanted to read from whatever source by whatever author. My mother hid only the Boccaccio, which I found dull anyway.

My writing career flourished in summer, mainly because my short stories were popular in the neighborhood. The kids would leave their jumping rope games to listen to the latest adventure of "The Human Car," based on my father's '28 Chevy. I also wrote my own versions of the Superman story with Lois Lane as the hero. I was confident of my powers, not yet dimmed by too much schooling. Later on, when teachers advised me to write about "what you know," I gave up my romantic tales and tried to be realistic. When I look at the success of popular romance and historical novels today, I wonder if I should have ignored that advice.

During adolescence, my diary became my constant companion and therapist, but in childhood I was a fiction writer. One of my earliest fantasies was of myself at age seven about to present my story to a New York publisher. The manuscript was rolled into a scroll and tied with a yellow ribbon.

Then there was my summertime newspaper, The Neighborhood Chronicle, published in our kitchen by the staff: my two best girlfriends, my little brother Tom, and me. We used "The Hectic Hectograph," a pan of viscous yellow jelly that had to be melted down after every edition of the paper and allowed to set before the next deadline. It would then be ready for our laborious news items about the neighbors, the neighbors' dogs, jokes, and a column, "Let's Go with Lythgoe."

I also tried my hand at mystery stories. This was fueled by the weekly radio show, "I Love a Mystery." I can see my mother now, nervously hovering over the Philco and wondering if she should just come right out and ban the program. She was afraid of nightmares, but I was being imprinted with a lifelong addiction to mysteries. In one of my own stories, I portrayed a seventh-grader locked in the school gym overnight. By investigating a trap door, she uncovered a gambling den which was operating under the auspices of the school's most popular teacher.

When I compare my childhood summers to those of my children, I realize that I tried to give them what I thought were the advantages of my own. I didn't dare let them wander in vacant lots or in the woods alone, but we certainly spent a lot of time at the library and in bookstores. With them, I learned to love *Charlotte's Web, The Little Prince,* Lloyd Alexander's *Prydain Chronicles, Harriet the Spy, Little House on the Prairie, The Great Brain,* and a host of delightful classics unavailable to my childhood.

For a long time, I believed that my love of reading could be partly attributed to a lack of television. But my children watched television, listened to rock music, went to the movies, and still became readers. Stephen is a reader and a writer of short stories. Lorraine is a reader, a poet, and a dedicated diarist. Scott, our most compulsive watcher of television, is also the most omnivorous reader. Yes, I exposed them to books in the womb and as soon afterwards as possible, but they outstripped me. Whereas I received a prize for reading "the most difficult book" in the tenth grade, *Les Misérables,* Scott's contribution to the tenth grade was a paper on T. S. Eliot. I didn't meet Eliot until college.

Who reads Victor Hugo anymore anyway? The other day I made a trip to the county library to see if the old volumes I read as a child were still there. Of course, Dickens, the Brontës, and Jane Austen were in their places, but many of the other romantic titles were being sold as discards for fifty cents apiece.

In my quest for idyllic summers, I find myself paradoxically expecting three months of productive writing and reading. I imagine gestation periods in the woods near my house, at my typewriter, at the beach. I expect to be transported back even though I know that as soon as I had my children, summer became the most difficult season for me. When they were on vacation from school, I was expected to take the full responsibility of work and play with them. Instead of finding time for myself and my dreams, I was living through my children and their books.

This was also hampered by the fabled Washington weather, which was nothing like the weather of my childhood. The inhuman humidity caused me to sympathize with Washingtonians who, b.a.c. (before air conditioning), would send their families away to the cooler lands from whence they came. One year we tried it. Chick drove Stephen, Lorraine, and me to Utah where we rented a married-student housing unit on the University of Utah campus. He stayed two weeks and flew back to Washington, leaving me with the car and the kids. I soon discovered that this was no fun. Not only did I have all the problems I had at home, but I was having them in a smaller space and without a partner. I also discovered that the much-vaunted dry heat of the West can beat down mercilessly and be just as oppressive as the hazy, humid heat of the East.

My children's summers took careful planning. I found myself spending time at the pool, even though I don't swim. I insisted that the children learn to swim, while I worked out at an exercise class for mothers. One year I discovered that Scott had been hiding out from his swimming lessons after I was out of sight. Obviously he had inherited my fear of the water, so I fished him out of the dressing rooms and made him start over. Meanwhile, Lorraine became a waterbaby and sun worshipper, a fact for which she now pays daily. It seems that during all those fun times in the pool and in our backyard, she was burning off the protective outer shell of her face. Now an umbrella and an ugly thick sunscreen are her constant companions in the sunshine.

Of course, we transported the children to the beach and to the Shenandoah, to Disneyland and Disney World, and to the World's Fair. We have shown them Europe from a camper bus, and we have even taken them on a Caribbean cruise.

Their summers were different from mine, more educational and more adventurous. And I am glad of that. It's just that now they are grown, I still expect summers to bring back the leisure of my own childhood and the chance to respond to the unassuaged creative child I was then. She nags at me—she seems to be asking me what has happened to all those stories and poems I was going to write.

[1986]

# VIRGINIA SORENSEN: A SAVING REMNANT

## I

**M**any years have passed since I, in searching for a thesis topic, began to read "Mormon novels." It seems odd to remember how electrifying were the forbidden Vardis Fisher and others I hadn't heard of: Richard Scowcroft, Maureen Whipple, Blanche Cannon, even Samuel Taylor. It must be a clue to my culture that a girl could get through graduate school as an English major without such an awakening, especially when many of those writers seem so harmless today. I wonder, along with Sam Taylor, if most of them were probably just "victims of bad timing." What my awakening consisted of was a realization that some of those giants from the Mormon historical past were human beings after all—in the words of Maureen Whipple, "saints by adoption."

I finally chose Virginia Sorensen as my subject because she was more diligent and more productive than other Mormon writers, because she was alive and still working, and because much of what she wrote made me wish I'd written it. I called my little work, "Virginia Sorensen: An Introduction."

It seems strange that several years later she should still need an introduction. Many Mormons who read have not read her, yet she is translated into many other languages. It is true that when she began to write, there were no independent Mormon publications like *Dialogue* and *Sunstone* to give her an appreciative audience. But the basic reason for her neglect stems, I think, from a misunderstanding many Mormons share about the purpose of fiction. Fiction has always been about sinners and their struggles, those struggles between good and evil which Dostoyevsky described as the battles of the human heart. Fiction writers must stand aside from that which most engages their personal lives, looking to a deeper engagement with their art.

At any rate, I take up my task again, with some changes in outlook, and perhaps with less objectivity. For the years have brought me a friendship with Virginia Sorensen, one which no doubt will exclude me from the company of the New Critics.

A western Mormon is a many-layered thing: a layer of history, a layer of geography, above all a layer of culture preserved in the old stories. Some of these layers are peeling off and disappearing, lost through quick conversions and puritanical notions from other religions, through a devastating urbanization, and through an ambitious materialism which touches all lives. New members seldom hear the old stories at all, except in sanitized versions. Having discovered Hector Lee's imitation of the late folk hero, J. Golden Kimball, I played the record for a group of Mormons. "He didn't say all those things," someone cried, while another pronounced it unfit for children. It was obvious that some were ashamed of that great character so recently with us. In a few years, all the "characters" will be lost if the writers among us don't act to preserve them.

*In Many Heavens* (1954), Virginia Sorensen describes "Old Brother Madsen, so old and bent his beard fairly reached his toes when he walked. Some folks objected to his sitting like a bum all day . . . but he always replied, 'I helped lay out this town and I'll sit in it where I damn please.'"

Virginia Sorensen represents a saving remnant of a remnant that should be saved. She writes of her ancestors, her grandparents, her parents, and herself in a way that preserves something of every western Mormon's personal history. In her works we have a special innocence, part of the fading murals which Mormon historians rush to save before zealous whitewashers have rubbed them away. As Wallace Stegner claims in his book, *The Sound of Mountain Water*, we are losing our connections to the past:

> In the old days, in blizzardy weather, we used to tie a string of lariats from house to barn so as to make it from shelter to responsibility and back again with personal, family, and cultural chores to do, I think we had better rig up such a line between past and present.

That many may not have read Virginia because of her penchant for reproducing people who suffer, sin, and die seems nothing short of blind anachronism. Any Mormon should appreciate her strong sense of history and place, her domestic love of the hearth, her celebration of love between man and woman, her rendering of the patterns of her background, with sympathy for those who must occasionally break the patterns to find themselves. But along with that, the childlike quality (in the biblical sense) of much of her work has won her two important awards in children's literature—The Child Study Award and the Newberry Medal—and has permeated her adult novels so that some, like *Kingdom Come* (1960) and *Where Nothing Is Long Ago* (1963), might well be called children's books for adults.

*Where Nothing Is Long Ago* is subtitled "Memories of a Mormon Childhood." It preserves the values of a childhood now lost, mine and Virginia's, so different from that of our children's.

## II

"How priceless it is," said Goethe, "when a human brain can reproduce what is mirrored in it." Virginia Sorensen began early to assimilate experience, storing it for good use. She began early to set her thoughts on paper. Her mother remembered that as soon as she could hold a pencil, she began to write "because she had to." Her Manti novels, *On This Star* (1946) and *The Evening and the Morning* (1949), attest to her ability to use the memories of her hometown. She lived in Manti until her high school years, dividing her reading and writing between the "22-ounce apple" tree in her front yard and the "house of my own" under the stairs in the Eggertsen home.

Even though her father was an inactive Mormon—a "Jack-Mormon" as she describes him in one of her stories—and her mother not a member at all, she was baptized and attended church meetings with friends. She listened to the old people and their stories until they became a part of her own memory. Her novels carry a load of these stories gleaned not only from memory, but from later readings in the diaries and journals of her ancestry.

The title story of "Where Nothing Is Long Ago" recalls a hometown killing over water rights. This same incident, somewhat changed, provides the climax to her Colorado novel, *The Neighbors* (1947). "People out west," she says, "remember when things were settled violently and they remember the dry wastes before the mountain water was captured and put to use."

Some characters appear and reappear. An apostate grandmother, described in *Where Nothing Is Long Ago,* all her life a rebellious feminist, insists on dying with her temple garments on. She is also the spirited heroine of *The Evening and the Morning,* Kate Alexander. An aunt who was once struck by lightning is recalled in *The Neighbors* and then given a story of her own, "The Teacher."

Virginia describes her aunt's reaction: "When she saw it, she nodded and said, 'It's all right, but so little. It's not one-hundredth the way it really was.' Which I thought a very good description of fiction in general. Lightning seldom strikes in words."

Virginia's first novel, *A Little Lower than the Angels* (1942), dramatizes the life of an ancestor who settled Nauvoo and died before the trek west. It also carries a romanticized version of Joseph Smith's love affair with Eliza R. Snow. A few years later, when Virginia read excerpts from a history of Scandinavian immigrants by William Mulder, she wrote him a letter:

> Your article in the *Utah Historical Quarterly* was so exciting that I immediately began getting ideas of how I must somehow do better. For years and years I have believed—for what reason I wonder, since I never really lived in the houses where the true tradition was but could only visit awhile, and listen, and pause always by the gate where I could hear and see it—that I was the one to tell this story you speak of. Almost I have heard the Call.

It was this call that sent her to Denmark to study the journals and the geography of her Danish ancestors, leading to that most missionary-minded of her books, *Kingdom Come.*

Sometimes she savors her stories so much that it interferes with her narrative, but in *Many Heavens,* set in a small northern Utah town just after the Manifesto, she seems to blend her best themes: scenery with history and personality, physical love with spiritual love, the excitement of learning with simple, domestic truths, the certainty of religious faith with the complexity of doubt. In short, this book blends Virginia's own peculiar people with her own particular art.

Here is her feeling for the small towns of her youth:

this valley . . . set like a particular jewel in the State of Deseret, where that State in the Union, and the Union in the great world flowed together . . . and a man, and his family, past, present, future, flowed together too.

Here is her feeling for her church as symbolized by the tabernacle in Salt Lake City:

all of these people were my people, the church my church, the huge vaulted roof over me a kind of personal possession, along with the golden wonder of the organ.

And her love of particular customs such as conference:

All the faces I saw seemed eager and glad and proud; people met with a hard Mormon handshaking, with splendid laughter, and so many warm greetings that the whole was like an immense overgrown church supper . . . for the missionaries had made Utah a gathering place from everywhere. It had its own peculiar melting in the great American pot. . . . As Neils always says, Conference is a tremendous portrait of the people at their best.

Throughout her books there are the beloved old people, like Billy Huckabee, who votes against the bishop every year for six straight years and plays "Kathleen Mavourneen" for the sacrament music. She speaks of the invisible freight of the immigrant, brought with them in their minds and hearts and in their ways of doing. She laments the dying of the old ones who took "all their lovely queerness" with them and left the valley the poorer.

She celebrates Mormon domesticity: "I needed the feeling of order in Leah's house, the washedness of her linen, the savory homelike tastes and smells that kept eating important in that house and so kept all the senses important along with it."

Virginia herself has always refused to hire a housekeeper because "there is a time with any project, large or small, when one becomes discouraged and quite certain it is all in vain and useless. At any rate, that always happens to me. Just now I'm housecleaning (which precious digging into corners and splashing suds to the elbows I would not give to any scrub-woman on earth, for it clarifies my immortal soul)."

Her books mirror her life—childhood in Sanpete County, Utah, college at Brigham Young University, and her marriage to a college professor, which led her to many parts of the country. She has had

Guggenheim Fellowships to Mexico and Denmark. She has also moved away from activity in the church; but as she moved "outside," her books gradually became more "inside." This is as one who leaves her home forever but looks back in pleasant nostalgia. In her dedication to *Where Nothing Is Long Ago,* it is a "dream dreamed out of memory."

When asked if she is a defender of the faith, she answers, "How could I be anything else? When we write of the things we know and love best, we cannot but be defending it to the world." To the white-washers and to others who object to some of her portraits, she would probably say with her Doctor Neils in *Many Heavens,* "Too many of us in this country expect to know just the sweet of everything. We bury half the truth of life in the privies back of the house. Under the ashes." And to those who think her too sweet, she can say with Zina, "If I am sentimental, then, all right, I am." The titles of her books state her aspirations: *A Little Lower than the Angels, On This Star, The Evening and the Morning, Kingdom Come, The Proper Gods.*

### III

In her traditions, western, rural, and tribal, Virginia Sorensen spins a "web of significance."

For writers, what is the lesson? The necessity for creating freely, certainly, but something more, the responsibility of preserving a web of significance men can live by. And this too is only a part—for it demands not only freedom within a tradition, but an ever-widening tolerance for the traditional values of others.

She perceives this web in the conflict of old and new, of sacred and profane, adjustment and estrangement, love and rebellion. Most of her characters must face inevitable conflicts without sacrificing their traditions. The Mormon culture provided her with a framework for developing her characters—growing up in a protected society, growing out into an unprotected and confusing world. As Zina says, "Not only had my mountains protected me, but had hidden much of the world from me, with its endless beauties and wonders."

Her non-Mormon novels and her children's books are thematically similar. Adan, of *The Proper Gods* (1951), must return to the protected Yaqui culture to reconcile newer philosophies with his ancient heritage.

The little Amish Esther in *Plain Girl* overcomes her envy for her well-dressed friend from the outside world to reaffirm not only friendship, but her own values. Many of Virginia's characters seem to say with Anne Morrow Lindbergh: "I mean to lead a simple life, to choose a simple shell I can carry easily—like the hermit crab. But I do not. I find my frame of life does not foster simplicity."

Mercy Baker, heroine of *The Angels*, is forever asking why. She accepts her husband's religion, not because she deeply believes it, but because she deeply loves her husband. She rebels against what she feels is the smug faith of simple believers, and she must face the frustration of polygamy. Chel Bowen, heroine of *On This Star*, has grown up with a strong faith, asking no questions, until she meets Eric whose desires work against her implacable surroundings. Rebelling with him brought her heartbreak at losing God too early, at a time when she still needed the sustenance of her belief.

Zina, the nurse-midwife of *Many Heavens*, though never actively rebellious, finds her life shaken out of its pattern by love for a married man. The ingenious solution to her problem echoes Emerson's statement, "Heaven is large and affords space to all modes of love and fortitude."

John, of *The Neighbors*, has rebelled against narrow modes of living. He believes in one thing—his right to think. He breaks away from the "self-conscious authority" in the mountains of Utah only to find the same insulated narrow-mindedness in the mountains of Colorado. The Yaqui man Adan rebels against his ceremonious life because it never changes. "I know it will be better to leave," he tells his sweetheart, "because I could never learn to accept everything." In the end, however, he reconciles the things he does not accept with those that he does.

The Mormon society, the Yaqui society, and the Amish have preserved their extreme individualism and their isolation only through the severest of tests. It is natural that such a struggle should give rise to groups of smug believers who refuse to see validity in other ways. In Mormon society, some feel that literature must express nothing but the highest and purest in an ideal culture. In reviewing Virginia's first book, John A. Widtsoe praised her gifts but deplored what he called "unlovely" incidents—as if all books must be "lovely."

Virginia treats smug believers with tolerance, sympathy and insight. In most of her stories, the guilty reach at least a partial realization of their mistakes. Zina vividly paints the self-righteous Stanley Widdeman, who "knew his proper spot in the great triangle with God at the top and the people at the bottom, the Word pouring downward to him through the authorities of Church and State, and his own word pouring downward to the members and officers below him. He was benign to the good child in his house . . . and quick to punish wrongdoing, so it would never get out of hand." How wrongdoing does get out of hand precisely because of his one-man crusade against sin provides an exciting denouement. Widdeman lives to repent of his blindness.

Most of Virginia's characters must give up their innocence, their sense of belonging, and then must somehow regain them in altered forms. In fact, characters in the Mormon novels are sometimes converted because the faith seems to offer a unity they once felt. Mercy's Simon finds happiness in the doctrines surrounding "family life, eternal family, the first family of God," wherein each would some day "achieve glory through this endless process of growing in his children." Adan comes to feel himself at one with the earth, like a tree, which gives him "a swelling of energy that made work good."

Some characters, however, are extremely conscious of the boundaries between people. Of these, Mercy Baker is most afflicted. The feeling of estrangement becomes most difficult when, through hard work and childbearing, she begins to lose both her beauty and her capacity for work.

It had occurred to Mercy in the first fear and uncontrollable anguish of knowing that she was caught within a body that refused to give her any longer what she desired from it, that perhaps she was old already, and that perhaps there was no real difference between sickness and age.

Virginia presents rebellion as a normal part of growing up and fitting into a mature society. Yet sometimes the most painful estrangement is the result of rebellion. Kate Alexander is Virginia's greatest rebel. Kate rebels in all ways and for this she suffers.

If you were a woman and a rebel, the only thing you could tear to pieces was your own life. So you turned upon yourself. There was no institution you could rend except at the place where it touched you; and so always you were the thing to be cut apart.

## IV

In a review of *On This Star*, Dale Morgan said, "One who feels that Mrs. Sorensen has larger capacity than the purveying of love stories closes the book with a feeling of sharp disappointment." Others have accused her of undue sentimentality. I must occasionally side with them, but in the end assert that she could do worse than purvey love stories. Through love stories she can write of women and their domestic problems, which she understands, and polygamy, which embodies so much of what is complex about love.

"You know how much of it is pride. If you change the things you are proud of, you change practically everything. The women who had the beginning of polygamy . . . they were the ones who had the worst of it, of course." The objection of Emma Smith made perfect sense to me. She knew people didn't understand, and she had to face them somehow.

When Zina decides to resolve her love problem in terms of polygamy, she does it after years of suffering. Mette, the first wife, explains that when a man loves two women and cannot have both, one will always be afraid and the other alone. "Why should all of us go on suffering so much?"

Before such conclusions may be reached, however, love must go through many stages. The first is the feeling of absolute privacy and oneness expressed by Virginia through Eliza R. Snow at Joseph Smith's first kiss:

> Then he took her and kissed her mouth with a passion that flowed into her and she knew for the first time the exquisite merging of herself with another.

In many ways, Virginia's view of love is typically patriarchal. Almost without exception, her women love their men as they love their god, looking for guidance, obeying "in righteousness," quite often mixing up the loving and the worshipping. This is expressed by a husband in *Kingdom Come* who describes his marriage: "Every time I go back to Hansine, it's better. Nothing but perfect communion with God himself can be compared to it, but I wondered if that was blasphemous when I first said it, but she told me . . . 'God is there,' she said, 'and he is there, Svend, in a good, true love. It's a kind of trinity for creation.'"

If the women in the novels see their men as gods, the men see their women as one with their surroundings, celebrating a love of place. Adan had these feelings about his Yaqui sweetheart: "Michaela belonged here in all ways, and he sometimes felt that her walk was beautiful because the street was familiar, every stone and the whole village and the people she met." Eric realizes that Chel turns "to the contours of the land like the sunshine itself." And Paul describes his wife in these words: "The pride of plain people was in Paulie; maxims made sense to her; children came easily from her body." Svend, the Danish missionary, hesitates to remove his sweetheart from her natural habitat: "She belonged where she was, bowing her head on the communion rail with her braids shining like metal, sipping wine in reverent silence from a silver cup, taking the Host from the white hands of the cassocked pastor in the reverent silence of an old church. She was right that if he loved her, he must belong in the same place." The need to belong, the sense of belonging in a church, in a place, in a heart are all important to Virginia's love stories.

When I first began work on my thesis, I meant to emphasize Virginia's universality and her realism, ignoring her regionalism. Today, I see her as a defender of the faith, a defender of the stories told by a people who have an inescapable dedication to a place and a history. She represents much of the Mormonism I was taught in my youth: a Mormonism that recognizes the human condition, that accepts different ways of seeing, a Mormonism that recognizes that true religion is not so much unity of opinion as unity of action. I admit to her womanly sentimentality, her love of particular places. In Wallace Stegner's phrase, I affirm her because she is "incorrigibly wholesome and life acceptant." I think she is probably speaking through her character Zina:

> I've got less and less religious in the organized sense over the years, but to this day, I can't think about the notion of sharing, about people who go out into it for whatever reason, the doctor, the missionary, priest, elder—anybody, without getting a feeling as wide and deep as a woman my size can hold. The really great ones got the fartherest out, reaching more and sharing with more. And the Greatest One was a friend to them all, born and unborn.

[1968]

# II
## Settling In

# MARRIAGE
# AND PRINTMAKING

My marriage is a process. And the name of the process is lithography. Lithography is based on the fact that grease and water do not mix. An image is drawn with crayon or lithographic ink on a prepared surface such as limestone. The surface is treated to make areas touched by crayon or ink receptive to printer's ink while blank areas are kept wet enough to repel the ink. At a visit to the show "Edgar Degas: The Painter as Printmaker," I learned that Degas worked with many printmaking processes during his lifetime—intaglio, etching, aqua-tint, drypoint, monotype—ending with lithography. The catalogue reports that "the process not the product captivated him." He would make a drawing and then start all over again. His repetitive images showed his fanatic obsession with the process. He often left the plate "unresolved" in what was obviously a very private medium for him, publishing his prints for only a few friends.

It couldn't be a better description of my marriage—a process that fascinates, a laboratory for growth, a travelogue, a history, a mystery story. A process in constant revision, some plates unresolved. A private process published only for a few close friends.

Recently a friend remarked that before she met me and my husband, she had assumed we would be "very much alike." But that was not the case, she said. "I found it very touching that two so different people could be so devoted to each other."

At ages twenty-nine and twenty-seven, Charles and I were ready for marriage. We had survived other romances and the weddings of most of our friends. We thought that we would make a good couple because we were both Depression-born babies with compatible family backgrounds. Because I was the eldest girl and he the youngest boy, we would mesh well. In fact, at the time, we thought we were very much alike.

We met as freshmen at the University of Utah, but we didn't date until seven years later after we both had obtained master's degrees, and he had finished a mission and his Ph.D. course work at Harvard. We were both teaching at BYU. Because he was an economics teacher and I an English teacher, we reasoned that he could balance our checkbook while I wrote home to his folks. We both had graduated from Lowell L. Bennion's courtship and marriage classes at the Institute of Religion. We had perfected his ABC dating method—date three people at the same time, each knowing about the others. We had also abided by Bennion's other dating principles—travel together (with chaperone) and enter into a secret engagement before announcing any intentions to the world. Though both secret and public engagements were brief, we were confident that we were beginning marriage with our eyes open.

Chick announced that, after finishing his dissertation, he planned to teach forever at the Lord's university. Because I, too, loved teaching there, I felt assured of a comfortable future close to home.

Three months later, we were on our way to Washingon, D.C.—for two years only, he promised—where he would work for Senator Wallace Bennett and finish his Ph.D. After, we would return, richer and wiser, to Provo and our building lot in Indian Hills. My Victorian upbringing had programmed me to follow my husband. I jumped the academic track and went.

Though I suffered acutely from separation anxiety (a ritzy term for homesickness), I am grateful now that we unconsciously followed another of Brother Bennion's bits of marital advice: move away from family immediately after marriage, returning only when your relationship is strong. Though Chick's aunt and uncle in D.C. and other friends were a real strength to us there, we were thrown mostly upon our own resources.

Moving away also gave us our first chance to notice how different we are from each other. For instance, he is a "morning person" like my father, who, entering my bedroom at 6:00 a.m., would break into "It's great to get up in the morning in the good old summertime" and throw the window open to the elements no matter what the weather. I, on the other hand, work better at night. If I can stay up beyond the phone's bedtime and sleep late the next morning, there isn't anything I can't do!

This has been a blessing. I can administer night feedings, and Chick can fix breakfast and officiate at morning seminary leave-takings.

Night and day are not the only things that we're as different as. He is a steady, even plodder, while I am a stop-start, spurt-rest type. We are still proving that morning tortoises can learn to live with evening hares.

On car trips, he makes a beeline for our destination with only brief pit stops, while I nag him into various detours. Traveling through Missouri, I insisted that we see Mark Twain's boyhood home in Hannibal. En route to the pageant in Palmyra, New York, I arranged a visit to Mark Twain's study, located in a gazebo on a college campus in Elmira.

Chick finally balked at all this literary sightseeing: "Next time I suppose that we will have to go looking for Mark Twain's bathroom." He teased me so much that I finally stopped begging him to veer off the highway to seek important landmarks. I did not, however, stop lecturing him on the rewards of the trip itself as opposed to narrowminded concentration on the destination.

Finally, on a trip to Boston, he suddenly left the highway at Hartford, steering purposefully to a house that I had seen only in pictures—Mark Twain's favorite and most imposing home, now the Mark Twain Museum.

Delighted at my surprise, he said, "I'm going to buy this house for our twenty-fifth wedding anniversary, just so you can sit in there and write the great Mormon novel." Chick's slow and sure temperament partly derives from an inherited physical disability that requires him to "take thought" of every step. This has taught him patience and durability. He has also developed a brand of fearlessness somewhat daunting to people with phobias like me.

In our first year together, I realized that I had married a man who had never done any reading beyond his professional and church assignments. Because reading is the thing I do best, we decided to make assignments to each other. While he read literary masterpieces like *1984* and *Brave New World,* I read an economic history, *The Worldly Philosophers.* Then we joined a Great Books club, where he responded with childlike joy to the adventures of Odysseus and the works of Dickens. I envied him. "I wish I had never read Dickens," I told him. "Reading him now would be a lot more fun than reading all those boring economists!"

Meanwhile, Chick taught me to love classical music, especially Handel's *Messiah,* a work he was trained to sing. When I informed him that I could not sing, he, refusing to believe me, requested that I accompany him to choir practice. After I had struggled through the first song, he turned to me and said, entirely without rancor, "You're right. You can't sing."

As the years passed, it became obvious that I am the kind of person who believes in speaking out and in talking out my problems. Chick is not averse to speaking out on points of doctrine from the pulpit and to the bearing of testimony, but sorrows and angers are best kept to himself. I believe that anger, as a normal human emotion, should be expressed and analyzed. His silence during moments of crisis could mean trouble. But through working and reworking, erasing and replacing, we represent two valid ways of thinking and feeling. This has led to certain compromises. Family home evenings have become a blend of the therapy sessions I want and the scripture lessons he wants. I also learned that his silence is not hostility but simply his habit of dealing with one thing at a time and meditating on it. Now he talks more; I talk less.

I was not aware that our differences were obvious until a friend called to confide her troubles. It seemed her husband's testimony was not strong enough to suit her. In fact, she had appointed herself guardian of her husband's faith. "I suppose that's the way it is with you and Chick," she said. "He's keeping you in the church." Insulted right down to my socks, I was less than polite as I told her that I considered my testimony every bit as good as his. Wasn't I born into the church, of goodly parents, and hadn't I been given a strong church education?

When Chick was made bishop and I became editor of *Dialogue: A Journal of Mormon Thought,* we installed the bishopric business on the main floor of our home and the *Dialogue* office downstairs on the basement level. This led to much lighthearted banter about "celestial-telestial" operations. Behind the banter, though, was the unspoken question, "How does the bishop get along with the editor?"

In the minds of some, piety and publishing don't mix—especially independent, scholarly publishing in a church context. But our response was: They do too mix! We had learned this at the Institute of Religion. Intellectuality and spirituality were two of the five ideals of

Lambda Delta Sigma, the church fraternity founded by Brother Bennion. We believed that truth needed no apology from scholars and thinkers who were carefully searching it out.

I was now aware that my husband and I were perceived as the quintessential liberal-conservative combination. The Liahona-iron rod dichotomy was applied to us.

About this time, we ran across this definition in the Leonard Arrington-Davis Bitton book, *The Mormon Experience*:

> Conservative Mormons include many highly-educated individuals who emphasize strong reliance on the wording of scripture, the authoritative structure of church government, and a church-centered social system. Liberals emphasize the boldness and innovative character of the Restoration, faith in the essential goodness of man and his possibilities of eternal progression, and the church's commitment to education and the resulting emphasis on rationality. The checks and balances are what give Mormonism both stability and progressivism.

I now think of us as the system of checks and balances for our family unit.

A couple of years ago, I was asked by the elders' quorum leader in our ward to speak at a fireside on the subject, "How can two people so obviously different find happiness? And how do these same people manage to rear three such gifted and outstanding children as Steve, Lorraine, and Scott?"

Finally mature enough to be flattered by the invitation, I began with this, "During the early, hectic years when the children were small, I used to wonder what would happen after they were grown and Chick and I were left to stare at each other—two aging, very different people. Whatever would we find to talk about? Well, as it turns out, we have exchanged enough traits over the years that our communication has improved. As we grow together, differences either fade or serve to keep us interested."

Then I described our rearing of what we laughingly called our "three only children." Born three years apart, with the girl in the middle, they often seemed to loathe each other as children. But our motto "Spend time with them when they are small, and they will spend time with us when they are tall" paid off. They are now good friends with each other and with us. I think the children provide a mirror image of what we once were like, recalling traits hidden under the sufferings of our mature years.

During the writing of this essay, I left it for a day or two in the typewriter, frustrated and blocked. Finally, I marched in with the intention of shifting it from machine to wastebasket. A note at the top of the paper stopped me, "Dear Mom, This is wonderful stuff. Hurry up and finish. Love, Steve." The note broke my block, and I was able to finish. But the process of my marriage is not finished. Just as some things are best left unsaid, we are, like Degas, leaving some of our plates creatively unresolved.

[1985]

# SEEDING IN

In fifth grade I read *Gone with the Wind*, deducing from it that if my father were to lie down by me at night, as he was wont to do during my frequent bouts with the croup, I would become a mother. I did not understand the mechanics of this miraculous event; I knew only that Scarlett had conceived immediately upon being carried up to bed by Rhett.

In those days the only helpful source of sex information seemed to be books. In high school Health II class, I was told that holding hands was an "unclean" practice. By the time Eugenics came along in my senior year, with its sketchy reproduction lecture, I had read everything I could lay my unclean hands on: Boccaccio, Kinsey, *Madame Bovary*, and an educational little book called *The Wonder of Life*.

My mother tells me that she considered herself well qualified to help "when the time came." Acting on advice that children should be answered only when they ask, she armed herself with a number of answers and waited. I armed myself with some questions and waited. I see us reaching blindly, never quite touching.

Finally, as I was making plans for college, Mother came to me for a heart-to-heart. I informed her gently that all her fine values had rubbed off on me, especially the talent for reading about the facts of life. She seemed relieved to hear it.

I recorded a few choice words about my sex education in my diary: "I emerged from Health II thinking that men were nothing but carnal animals and it would be dangerous to hold hands with them. Kissing could only lead to a drastic case of syphilis. It never occurred to our old-maid teacher that men could be people like us with intelligent minds. They were just bundles of passion." Then I added, "The truth is, I can never quite connect the boys I know to the description in those so-called sex education lessons. Men are always people to me."

Nowadays we are told, in dark tones, that children are learning about sex in the streets. As a child, I played in vacant lots and orchards where I often conversed with my peers, but I don't remember gleaning any useful sex information. I dimly remember, at age four, sharing an anatomy lesson behind the bushes with an older man who was six. Adults weren't much help either. They made the whole thing sound dangerous enough to strike fear into the heart or so sacred that it defied expression.

One night as I sat in our ward MIA, a young leader announced in bored tones that next Wednesday night would be Rose Night for the Mia Maids. I got a sudden gust from my past. I smelled all those chaste Rose Nights when we girls, dressed in our best, chose a particular rose to represent our standards. I had known that the roses had something to do with sex, something about being beautiful and smelling clean that seemed far removed from the excited, sweaty feeling that comes over you when you are with a boy you like.

But I grew up in halcyon times. It was okay for me to learn about life through reading until I reached the University of Utah and the Institute of Religion. I learned then that, although romantic love was nice, friendship with your partner was the only way to get through an eternal marriage.

Values were presented in a new context for me. Kissing is not in itself bad; a woman's body is not just a machine for turning out children. It was a calm approach. There was no hurry. So I waited until I had earned two degrees before I decided to get married.

Nowadays children know too much too soon—or do they? A few years ago, I took our eleven-year-old son to a movie which I had been led to believe was safe for mothers. One scene made me squirm. Just as I was getting ready to send Stephen for popcorn, he whispered, "Relax, Mother, I know all about it." I wanted to ask in my waspish voice, "What do you know?" but the hushed theater hardly seemed the right place.

I am grateful to the church for keeping my son and other children busy and giving them wholesome friends. But they have other friends and influences light years away from the world I grew up in. I cannot police their world; I do not want to try. But I do want to live with them, and I don't want them to think sex is too sacred or too scary. How can I tell them that it is also playful and jolly and sad and strenuous and relaxing and loving?

Sometimes it is coming together to make life; sometimes it is clinging together against death. I don't want my teenagers to think of sex as
just a dangerous temptation, like drugs, instead of what it is, the motivating life force that enables us to be both different from each other
and alike too.

Many Mormons have objected to sex education in the public
schools. What do they offer instead? Vague instructions about teaching
children in the home. By what guidelines? And where should these be
published—in the Sunday School and Relief Society manuals? In the
*Church News?*

The discovery of the Gladstone journals in England a few years ago
made the point that Victorians writing about sex in their diaries often
used a code language obscure to us but perfectly understood by other
Victorians.

Writers of church manuals and editorials sometimes use code language confusing to young people and grown-ups, too. In a seminary discussion, my daughter, age fourteen at the time, responded to a comment
made by her seminary teacher that "living together before marriage is a
sin" with the statement that she thought it a good idea. The couple could
get to know each other before taking the big step. By nightfall, word
got around the ward that the bishop's daughter was dangerously liberal.
When we questioned her about it, I was sorry I didn't have a camera
to catch her puzzled and innocent expression. She had understood the
words literally, with no idea that they were sexual euphemisms.

When we speak in code language, when we use vocabulary from
Victoria's time or from biblical sources, we need to provide a dictionary.
Some Relief Society lessons made an admirable attempt to deal with
important questions children ask about sex. But the $64,000 question
produced only that hoary quotation from the Bible: "And they [sic?]
twain shall be one flesh." I try to imagine how that might sound to the
literal minded—Siamese twins? I may be making light of sacred things,
but surely it is possible to find in all our rich language some words that
are both inspiring and informative.

An editorial in the *Church News* suggested a return to the Days of
Chivalry. Its author lamented the passing of a "golden age" when men
were gentlemen and ladies were "feminine, modest, virtuous, intelli-

gent, well-groomed and mannerly." Unlike the writer, I was not alive when knighthood was in flower, but I know that I live in a day when the nights are full of hoods seeking to deflower modest, intelligent, well-groomed ladies. And I don't think such editorials do much to protect them. Recent rape reports show that even modest, virtuous women are attacked, sometimes by men who know them and who themselves look presentable. In fact, such rape is usually a violent criminal assault having little to do with sex or with grooming.

I certainly do worry about arming my daughter and my sons. How much information will help without frightening them? What can I say that will teach them to love and protect their bodies without thinking of their bodies as a come-on to crime? I am not suggesting that church publications be indelicate or crude, only that they be clear.

We hear about families at every turn, but nowhere do we learn how families are made. The family home evening manual seems a logical place to tell the story. We could learn how bodies are made, how wonderfully made, with lessons on the right names for the parts. I would guess that many grown-ups are still woefully ignorant of their bodies and their best care. Many Mormons cannot bear to hear the right names for the private parts even when pronounced in the hospital. In fact, children may well know more about their bodies than their parents do and keep silent in deference to the embarrassment they so easily sense. And we, the parents, are not sure what values they are soaking up. We know they are interested in sex, probably more than in any other subject, except for basketball, of course. I know, because one summer I had the misfortune of teaching a class at an LDS youth conference opposite a Mormon obstetrician. I was discussing television and the media; he was discussing sex. I had three people in my class; he had everybody else. Many Mormons have now qualified themselves in the helping professions that include sex education. Surely their talents could serve us.

We could even employ proxy experience—literature. Family counselors could join with teachers and parents to create lessons using stories and poems that deal with sexual relationships. Families and classes could air their feelings while focusing on the situations of fictional characters in a non-threatening way.

A book I read long ago, whose title slips me now, told the story of a young girl believed to be feeble-minded. Since she lived on a farm with her grandmother, nobody worried about her until her grandmother died. While the courts tried to decide what to do with her, they discovered she could read. This led to an examination that proved her difficulty was not mental but physical—cerebral palsy. Thrilled by his sister's newly discovered intelligence, her brother brought her several novels with lurid covers. In a touching scene, she picks up one book after another, and puts them down with the words, "They just don't sound right." Her grandmother had called it "seeding in"—teaching her to read the Bible and other "good books" so that lesser works wouldn't attract her.

A friend, a former bishop, tells me he hopes his children will not come to him with questions about sex. He thinks the less said the better, the less they know, the less he knows that they know, the less discomfort all around. Though this was partly in jest, I think his view is secretly shared by many. Is ignorance really the best protection?

As I write, I hear my daughter talking to her father in the study. She sounds angry. "But," she is saying, "they never give us any reasons! They just talk about how bad it is!"

His voice floats gently down the hall. I catch only certain words like "clean" and "holy" and "marriage is the most important," and I sympathize with him. We have agreed about the danger of euphemisms like "clean" and "unclean," about the danger of thinking sex is dirty for the first twenty years of life and expecting it to be washed clean and made holy overnight by marriage.

How would I talk to her then? Certainly my long childhood, with its books and classes, would avail me little. She has read the right books, and I have answered her questions as honestly as I could. She has listened in church, no doubt hoping for magic words to unravel once and for all the mystery. It isn't that she hasn't heard the reasons for chastity. Perhaps her anger comes from our inability to say what we really feel.

Describing feelings is, after all, so very difficult. Our children don't even use the same terms we used, like "petting" and "necking." And trying to describe emotions somehow seems to cheapen them. Putting emotions into words brings them outside, in the open where people can paw through them. It somehow seems better to keep emotions inside, where they can stay safe and warm.

I realize that one's feelings can only be incarnated in an atmosphere of trust, of "positive reinforcement" and "feedback," to use modern parlance. Have we created that atmosphere in home and church? Do we know what meanings our children are taking from our words and actions?

The time has come to find out. I head toward the study. Perhaps I can start by admitting that I too am confused.

I hesitate outside the door, and then I knock.

[1972]

# MY CHRISTMAS DISASTERS

**W**hy is it that the mere thought of Christmas can turn an otherwise intelligent Dr. Jekyll into someone who should be Hyde? I am referring, of course, to those domestically inept folk who wouldn't be caught dead with needle and thread during the year but at the Christmas season suddenly think they can wax artsy-craftsy.

As a teenager, the only thing I ever did with my hands, besides lift bon-bons to my lips, was to crochet fascinators. Fascinator—a cleverly worked triangle in the lovers' knot stitch, to be worn around the head in such a way that the point of the triangle rests between the brows, as in a Spanish mantilla. The lovers' knot stitch was an open, romantic web. Picture me at fifteen, sitting on our front step, madly crocheting and watching for someone fascinating to come down the pike. I have no idea how many fascinators I created as gifts for friends and family. Fortunately, none are extant.

The temptation to become artsy-craftsy overnight didn't really hit me, though, until I was safely married and a mother. Then everything seemed suddenly possible!

First, there was the year of the cookie.

I, who have always considered cookies as nothing more than failed cake, who cannot think of a worse waste of time than to stand for hours dropping dollops of dough onto burned-over metal sheets, found myself seized with a desire to do some creative baking. So, with my handy little drawing pen and a large piece of cardboard, I proceeded to draw freehand none other than the characters from "The Twelve Days of Christmas"—the partridge, the drummer, the lord, the swan . . .

After I had finished cutting them out, I mixed up a huge vat of dough, along with suitable pots of decorative frosting. I intended to make twelve dozen cookies for twelve lucky friends. But the dough seemed to grow as my energy diminished. I ended up, not with twelve dozen cookies, but with twelve slightly deformed gargoyles peeking out from the crannies of Notre Dame. Naturally they were too precious to give away to someone who could callously eat them, so I saved them until they crumbled of their own accord.

Did that experience tip me off, thus saving me from future disasters? Hardly.

The next year I designed my own Christmas cards. But did I simply design one and have it printed with a poem inside? No, I couldn't do that. It would have been both sane and reasonable. I created a different card for everyone on my list: Christmas trees, Christmas poems in the shape of Christmas trees, short jingles, and long doggerel. The kindest response to all this activity was this: "Even though I couldn't read your card, I thought it was nice."

Never one to make the same mistake twice, I went on to a different mistake. The next year, everyone was into decoupage. A friend of mine had a whole decoupage studio in her basement. In fact, it had become a way of life with her. Fall down, and you were liable to end up on a vase.

She was only too eager to instruct me—two weeks before Christmas—as I determined to make antique maps for four close friends. We had a wonderful time, she and I, gossiping and polishing, cutting and painting, gluing and solving the problems of our misspent childhoods. But, when the two weeks were up, I was the proud possessor of one map of the ancient walled city of Paris. I wrapped it up and gave it to myself. Who else would appreciate so many hours of labor—especially when the whole thing lifted and bubbled the minute I transported it from her cool basement" to my warm house.

You probably think by now that I had entirely forgotten my past love affair with the fascinator. No such luck. One day when a friend admired my shawl, one my mother had worked in the lovers' knot stitch and given me years before, I thought to myself: "I remember that stitch; I will surprise my friend."

When I sank down in front of the fire with my crochet hook, my yarn, and a decorative box to hold everything, my family was amazed. I became an inscrutable Madame DeFarge, working day and night, refusing to divulge the secret of my industry. Voila! After only sixteen days, I stood triumphantly and tried on my lovers' knot shawl: a fit muffler for O. J. Simpson!

Ever on the alert for ways to involve the children in Christmas decorating, I hit upon a scheme. I would outline their bodies in felt. They would lie down and I would draw around them; then they could decorate their own silhouettes with old clothing scraps, and the result would be a wonderful wall hanging. Well . . . it would have been easier to hang up the children.

Some people go wild over Christmas trees. Their artsy-craftiness is kindled at the potential of a giant blue spruce. Never mind that they live in a one-bedroom apartment where the ceilings hit just above the ears. Nothing will do but to search hill and dale for the perfect tree.

I had been finding my perfect tree at a certain church lot for several years. Legend had it that the trees were cut fresh from mountaintops and brought down into the valley on the fifteenth of December, no sooner, no later. In order to nab one of the ten blue spruces in the load, you had to arrive before dawn on the fifteenth and huddle in your cold station wagon until the gate swung open and the eager throng battled its way in.

Alas, came the year when our tree man announced that the blight had reached the spruces before he could. No spruces this year. My friend, who was driving the station wagon, talked me into a mere pine. So we loaded one for me and one for her and started for home.

On the way we spotted, tied to a post in lonely splendor at another lot, a single blue spruce. I couldn't resist. I leapt out, paid for the tree, and loaded it into the wagon. The car was now so full of trees, with one sliding out the back, that I positioned myself among the branches, perched like a chubby partridge, and clung there until we reached home.

What to do. I now had two huge trees, one for upstairs, one for downstairs. I called another of my deranged friends, who is perfectly reasonable at other times but who, at Christmas, goes around feeding trees from a specially mixed brew of maple syrup and boiling water. She set up both of my trees, and my family decorated them while singing carols and drinking cider.

The next morning, while going about my housewifely duties, I thought I detected a gentle shudder from the direction of the spruce.

I paid no attention. There it was again, a sound almost inaudible to anyone who has not developed failsafe hearing from listening for baby breath in the night. That's what it sounded like—a gentle intake of breath. As I drew closer, I knew what it was—needles dropping to the floor and snuggling deep into our plush carpet. I rushed downstairs to check the pine. It was doing the same thing. Our fresh trees were dropping their needles with abandon.

This year, I don't care what anybody says—I'm decorating the dieffenbachia!

[1969]

# DIET DIALOGUE

Now that summer is here, it is time for a diet dialogue between myself and my sylph.

*Self:* Why is it that even though I have placed a picture of a Vogue dress on the refrigerator door, I have just opened that same door and wolfed down a generous pot of potato salad?

*Sylph:* Because you put the picture on the door. It called attention to the door. You long ago learned to resist the motivation of Vogue.

*Self:* But I want a new dress for summer. Isn't that motivation enough?

*Sylph:* No. In your heart of hearts, and underneath those layers of fat, you think that somewhere there is a dress that will make you as glamorous as if you were thin.

*Self:* But I really am trying! I heard that most fatties eat too fast, so by setting the stop watch and chewing every mouthful twenty-three times, I managed to slow down to ten minutes. How can I reach the forty-five minutes that diet doctors suggest?

*Sylph:* By eating more food.

*Self:* Thanks a lot! You're a big help!

*Sylph:* Helpful, yes. Big, no.

*Self:* Come out of there, I say!

*Sylph:* Not until you stop stuffing and start stiffening.

*Self:* I want to know why I can't be satisfied with one treat at a time? Why can't I stop at one M & M?

*Sylph:* Because sugar breeds a desire for sugar.

*Self:* But I do it with bread and yogurt and everything else!

*Sylph:* You are feeding not the hunger of the body, but the hunger of the soul.

*Self:* Don't get pious with me, Sylph!

*Sylph:* What I mean is: you eat to keep from doing something important with your talents.

*Self:* I have noticed that when I am scared about something I have to do, like introducing a bill on the floor of the Senate or opening on Broadway, I can't eat.

*Sylph:* Most people function best when just a little hungry. Not dying of malnutrition, you understand, just a little hungry.

*Self:* The question then becomes, how can I stay scared?

*Sylph:* By looking in the mirror all the time.

*Self:* You don't have to insult me! I also find that when I try to concentrate, I want to eat.

*Sylph:* Your body tries to sabotage your mind. Try the smell of rotten apples in your desk.

*Self:* Rotten apples?

*Sylph:* What worked for Schiller might work for you.

*Self:* Was he thin?

*Sylph:* No, but he was a great German poet. Maybe you could be one too.

*Self:* Sylph, you mock me!

*Sylph:* No, I am a mock-up of you, a thin version of you, and I can't come out until you stop clogging my doorway with food.

*Self:* I have founded my own little Diet-of-the-Month Club—every month a new diet. Why won't a diet do it?

*Sylph:* Your problem is not finding the right diet. It's not wanting to diet.

*Self:* I do want to diet! Why do you think I am so miserable? Of course I want to diet!

*Sylph:* No. You want to lose weight, but you don't want to diet. You are a spoiled, self-indulgent . . .

*Self:* Stop! I am trying to be healthy. Why, I have been buying my snacks at the health store instead of the pastry shop. Why can't I lose on pumpkin seeds?

*Sylph:* Because you eat 5,000 of them!

*Self:* I have heard people say that those who don't like to eat don't like to do anything else either. They aren't even sexy. Wouldn't I rather be sexy?

*Sylph:* Is fat sexy?

*Self:* Why isn't it possible that I like to eat just because food is good? Must I be suffering from suppressed hatred of my mother or fear of the world or something awful like that?

*Sylph:* No, but isn't it possible to enjoy it half as much? Do you have to gobble up everything on the plate and then chew on the porcelain?

*Self:* Stop! You're right. It's a question of will.

*Sylph:* When will you begin? Why not declare a Fast Day, not just once a month but once a week?

*Self:* On Fast Day I eat the same as I do on every other day, except that I eat it faster.

*Sylph:* You' re impossible!

*Self:* Okay, okay, I want to be thin, but not badly enough. What should I do?

*Sylph:* I don't know, but if I don't get out of here soon, you'll forget all about me. Remember how you cried when the scales hit 115? Remember how you felt when you were four months pregnant and weighing in at 129? Now, think how happy you were last year when you got back down to 140. You may just escalate me right into the grave, if you pardon the mixed metaphor.

*Self:* Okay, I promise you this, Sylph—I will let you out very soon . . . right after Christmas!

[1985]

# THE HOURGLASS FACTOR

Since my husband Charles and I had grown up in Utah, we naturally assumed that our well-honed prejudices about the effete East as compared with the golden West were genetic. When we moved to Washington soon after our wedding, we vowed to return to the West after amassing a small fortune—enough to build on our lot in Provo's Indian Hills. After all, we would be following in the footsteps of certain heroes from our Mormon past—hardy politicos like Senator Reed Smoot who had been willing to exile themselves temporarily for the good of their country. Fortunately, Charles's position as legislative assistant to Senator Wallace Bennett meant frequent trips to Utah, and it was on one of these that our first child Stephen was born. I remember thinking that further trips would prepare Stephen for the time when he, as a son of BYU faculty, would inherit all the perks and privileges of that exalted station.

But the lure of the capital proved too strong. Charles succumbed to another job offer in Washington, so this time we bought a house and grew another child. Our exile seemed complete. We had joined the host of other Utah transplants who had migrated to D.C. thinking to stay one, two, three, or five years and had stayed into the second generation of Marriotts, Puseys, Foulgers, and Knudsons.

Though we gave in gracefully to our fate, we were comforted by the thought that at the appropriate time our children would return to BYU for their education. We say "return" because even though our first two children had lived in Utah only nine months, we were sure they would think of Utah as their home. The Washington area boasts excellent universities and a large Mormon support group, but we ignored all that. Our Mormon children would attend "the Lord's university."

Our children did attend BYU, and their experiences there have taken the shape of an hourglass: as they graduate from high school they leave behind an open, urban society, but upon entering the university they encounter what they perceive to be superficial constraints, stifling standards, and a narrow protectionism appropriate to the mountain-ringed valley. It is as if they have to funnel through this narrow passage in the glass before their worlds open out again.

As we drove to Provo one warm August day to deposit our firstborn in a Helaman Halls cubicle, we assured ourselves that he would have no trouble adjusting. We were wrong. Yes, Stephen liked the mountains, but if he couldn't have a car to drive, if he couldn't go dancing in places where they played "funky" music, or meet girls who looked like real people rather than models, he would just as soon have himself committed to the Missionary Training Center. In time his mission did come. We attributed his joy to his commendable religious zeal, but I now believe it was derived, in part, from his relief at leaving BYU.

Lorraine's suffering was greater than Stephen's. Though she had fortified herself by taking with her three roommates from Virginia, she, too, found the atmosphere debilitating. Choosing to live in Heritage Halls so she could cook her own meals, she found many of the young women in the dorm spent the better part of their lives fixing candlelit dinners for fellows they hoped would give them the right to blow out more candles at ritual "candle-passing," ceremonies. Branded a "liberal easterner," chastised for wearing hats and refusing to sew up the slits in her skirts (actually she hadn't learned to sew), she reported that young men first made fun of her accent, then of her opinions, but always attempted to kiss on the first date. For several years the only Mormon in her class in high school, Lorraine was disappointed to find that at BYU she was still "different."

By then we were asking ourselves whether eastern children of western parents could find happiness at BYU and allowed Lorraine to write away for catalogues from other universities. When she saw the price tag on the courses, her enthusiasm wavered enough for us to make a suggestion. Since Stephen would be returning from Spain and Scott would be graduating from high school, she might want to be with them at BYU. "I know you weren't expecting to be tested there at the Lord's university," I told her, "but life is always a test. That's the name of the game." She had admitted to liking her classes, her teachers, and her roommates—what more could she ask?

About this time I received a letter from a friend in Provo who had observed Lorraine's behavior on campus. "She has a chip on her shoulder about westerners," he reported. "She's always talking about, 'Molly Mormon' and 'Bobby BYU.'"

So Lorraine returned another year, this time to an honors science class and a London semester abroad. She also overcame a longstanding fear of auditions—a real problem for a dancer—and was accepted into the International Folk Dancers. The science class filled the gap in her background and was so exciting that she wrote about the caring way the professors motivated her to study.

Her letters from London reported ecstatically the fading of her fears at living far away and the opening of personal frontiers: "I am really interested in history now. I don't know why I hated it so in high school. I also like going to museums. My classes are the best I have ever had. The problem is that I am now interested in so many things I don't think I'll ever be able to decide on a major."

When I visited her in London during her last three weeks there, I was delighted to see the mother-daughter tables turned. She was holding my hand to cross the street, directing me through the intricate subway system, introducing me to her favorites in the Tate Gallery, slipping me in to see *Nicholas Nickleby* and *Cats* on student rush tickets. I joined her and the rest of the group for a literary tour of King Arthur-Shakespeare-Hardy-Fowles country. I realized then that my "liberal easterner" had become a delighted citizen of the world. And as for Molly Mormon and Bobby BYU, they had metamorphosed into real people. In an essay for her English class, she spoke of her change in attitude and her growing love for her fellow students no matter their origins, hairstyles, or speech patterns.

When the time came for Scott to leave for BYU, we found him harder to part with—not that we loved him more, only that he was our last child and had graduated from high school a year early. I was afraid his adjustment would be more painful than that of his siblings. He had grown up practically undisturbed in a lair we lovingly referred to as "the pit." His bedroom on the basement level opened onto a large family room, giving him unlimited access to books, typewriter, television, telescope, and the Top Forty. In college he would have no space to spread out, and some of his habits were certain to be frowned upon.

He was inclined to distribute his papers and clothing wherever he saw fit, invite all and any comers to dance to his record collection, and bake giant cakes in the middle of the night.

Encouraged by lengthy letters that led me to believe he was either homesick or had overcome his hatred of letter writing, I was again made apprehensive when I visited him on campus.

I arranged to meet him at the candy counter in the Wilkinson Center. My heart hurt as he strode up, a foot or two taller and several curls shorter. His hair had been mercilessly shorn, exposing his ears to the winter winds. He was not wearing a coat, only a bright orange, tattered windbreaker with the words, "Virginia Cavaliers," inscribed thereon. He was wearing his roommate's shoes because his own had given up the ghost.

On the way to the shoe store, I inquired after his winter coat. "It's a nuisance. I just put on more layers." But where were these layers? I was suddenly overcome with remorse. Why hadn't I prepared him better for the rigors of Utah? The way he inhaled the spaghetti at Marie Callender's made me doubt that he was being properly fed. He looked thin. An image of him as a child suddenly spun through my mind, the memory of his determined independence along with his seeming fragility. Scraps of a poem I had written about him when he was a youngster of five floated up: "walks out alone / his body enough to shelter him / from rain and other agonies." I remembered, too, the troubles of his fifth-grade year, when sick stomachs and tears caused me to investigate his class and his teacher. His teacher was kind; the classroom was pleasant; life looked easy for a child. Frustrated, I asked him, "Scott, what is it you want?" He snapped back indignantly, "I want an education! That's what I want!"

Was he finding what he wanted at BYU—an education? He said, yes, his classes were suitably challenging. He had often met with his brother and sister to discuss issues presented in his science and religion classes. His English class had helped him overcome his dislike of writing. His honors colloquium had convinced him that he really was in college, where people collected evidence, stated ideas, and were challenged to think. Although he felt constricted in some ways, he had to concur with Stephen that "the teachers at BYU are as good as any in the world, so if you want an education, you can get it."

Later all three of the children agreed that almost without exception their teachers had placed their students first—even before the publish or perish syndrome, even before salary requirements. Although Lorraine had suffered from the marriage-mindedness of the social scene, her caring teachers and helpful friends, and her experiences in Europe had convinced her that BYU was a university with its doors opened upon the world.

Now that Stephen and Lorraine are seniors and Scott is well into his sophomore year, I sense that my children have passed through the narrow neck of the glass. As they have grown in understanding, they have begun to recognize the constrictions of their own hearts. And as their education has launched them on new adventures of mind and spirit, geographical boundaries have disappeared, prejudices have faded. The hourglass has widened once again.

[1982]

# PILLOWS OF MY FAITH

One day I received a long-distance call asking me to participate on a panel called "Pillars of My Faith." Because of a faulty connection, I heard "pillows" of my faith. After a hearty chuckle, I realized that I liked "pillows" better. Pillars can crumble in a quake or be toppled by a hirsute Sampson, whereas pillows can comfort, support, and sandbag against disaster. Of course, pillows can be mashed, run over, and otherwise rendered useless by the stresses of life. But faith is not synonymous with certainty. As Lowell L. Bennion puts it, "Faith is not cut and dried, is not fixed and static, but is something as dynamic as life itself."

Admitting that a metaphor can break down as quickly as the stuffing of a pillow, I organized my thoughts around pillows that comfort and heal, bolsters that translate into the principles I live by, and sandbags that barricade against the ravages of time.

## I

I was the first child of parents who taught me to believe in miracles and gifts of the Spirit. After all, I was a "miracle baby." Shortly after my birth, I was saved from death by a bishop who arrived after the doctor had given up on my little blue body. Bishop Howick was known for the gift of healing, and it was understood that I had been spared in order to develop worthwhile gifts of my own. In our comfortable home on an acre of fruit trees with room for cows and chickens, I looked to the ring of mountains beyond our yard for safety and inspiration.

With my parents and siblings, two brothers and a sister, I went to church in a comfortable ward that included a band of cousins who accompanied me all the way through high school. Though my parents had little formal education, they encouraged their children to go as far in school as their austere budget would allow and our own efforts could supplement. My diary records that, after working for a year after high school, I was barely able to cover the first quarter's tuition at the

University of Utah. When I burst into tears at the thought of quitting until more money could be found, my father exclaimed, "You're going back to school if I have to rob a bank!" Then he turned to Mother with the words, "What's fifty dollars if she's going to be unhappy?"

Such a large sum for those days—the early 1950s—and such strong family support! This brought me to some remarkable teachers and mentors at the university and the LDS Institute of Religion across the street. Contrary to dire rumors about loss of faith through the influence of godless professors, my studies only quickened my faith. Later in graduate school, my thesis chairman, Bill Mulder, would persuade me to choose as my subject a living Mormon novelist, Virginia Sorensen. Bill and Virginia were no longer active in the church, but their integrity and high standards of scholarship harmonized with my faith. Virginia was courageous enough to write about her Mormon background in a way that helped me to understand my own. I also came to know the work of other Mormon writers. I had been taught to respect the "revelations" of others, and these writers were revelators in their own way. Through them, I learned that the great pioneers of my cultural and religious history had been struggling human beings like me. It seemed, then, that even so humble a soul as mine could aspire to good works.

At the Institute I joined the church fraternity, Lambda Delta Sigma, which was dedicated to the ideals of fellowship, leadership, spirituality, intellectuality, and cultural life. I also took classes in everything from world religions to courtship and marriage. In the seven years I spent there, I was exposed to T. Edgar Lyon's unfailing devotion to honest history, to George Boyd's challenging dedication to scholarship, and to Lowell Bennion's quiet consecration to Christian service. In fact, Lowell, or "Brother B.," as we called him, came to symbolize all the pillows of my faith. Even today, the still, small voice of my conscience often speaks in his voice. Through his teaching, his writing, and his counseling, I caught a glimpse of my place in the scheme of things. Through his "work parties" and service projects that took us out into the community and beyond ourselves, I began to accept responsibility for my own life. It was then that I formed the notion that the church was "my" church, that it belonged not only to its leaders, but also to me.

When I finally departed from the university and the Institute, it was for another safe place.

As an instructor in English at Brigham Young University, I found a stimulating circle of friends. The Mormon students were easy to teach because of our shared values, but they were also challenging to teach because of their high expectations. I felt fortunate. I was being paid for what I loved to do.

Also at BYU was a young man I had met at the Institute, Charles Bradford, a returned missionary, now working on his Ph.D. and teaching economics. We saw a chance to test Brother B.'s courtship advice. It worked. When we married in the temple, Brother B. gave us the use of the Institute building as a wedding gift for the evening's reception. After teaching one more semester at BYU, we departed for Washington, D.C., where Chick took a position on the staff of Utah's senator Wallace F. Bennett. My long childhood was over, and some of my pillows were hardening into the bolsters of my maturity.

## II

I see now that, during my early years, my pillows were mainly people. Joseph Smith's declaration, "If my life is of no value to my friends, it is of no value to me," was my motto. Although the scriptures warned against putting faith in the arm of flesh, I went ahead and trusted a whole host of people. This trust did not displace my faith in God but reinforced it. Many of my fellow-men and women combined the best male-female traits that I have always attributed to God.

Because my father was a nurturing man and because I had been influenced by a number of other nurturing men, it was difficult for me to think of God the Father as angry and unapproachable. At the Institute, Brother Lyon described Joseph Smith as a father who sometimes missed church meetings to minister to a sick child. My own father had been gentle and responsive in the same way.

My teachers were nurturing too. Their message was that God is good, that he isn't the scary, all-powerful calvinist of other religions, that he operates under the same laws that bind his children. Relationships with brothers and boyfriends and then with my husband gave me reason to trust the male of the species.

I began to read widely in a new field—women's studies. Mormon scholarship was beginning to recognize the contributions of our pioneer foremothers, thanks to Leonard Arrington and his colleagues at the Church Historical Department. As I read the first women's issue of *Dialogue* and the new women's newspaper, *Exponent II,* I began to think of myself as a full-fledged Mormon sister. I gained a testimony of the integrity of women who are willing to share their own gifts of the Spirit.

As for my earthly mother, I believe I had so internalized my mother's influence on me that I was grown up before I could understand her as a separate person. Then I appreciated her unwavering devotion to her family and to her god. Because of this, I moved easily into friendships with female cousins and neighbors and on to lasting friendships with other women.

By then I had accepted the Mormon concept of God as a being in history and in some way limited by law. This led to a paradox. God is far higher than I, with powers that surpass understanding, and yet He is not responsible for death and evil. This makes Him much more than a cosmic real estate broker whose main duty is to dispense kingdoms to the worthy. Nor is He like a giant puppeteer who plucks people off the earth at inconvenient times for unclear reasons. Nor is He a kind of entrapment officer working to catch the unwary. In fact, I am able to love and worship Him because of the free agency that grows from my pre-mortal spirit.

This faith in my creator became my bolster. Along with this I formed a respect for authorities. "We shall always need authorities to guide us," says Brother B., "but we must test their right to lead us. This we can do through thought, experience, and revelation." My respect for authority and my desire to learn from authorities in school and church does not cloud my respect for my own free agency. I am comforted by the concept of division of labor. I have my job; you have yours. We are required to seek our own revelation. If your revelation contradicts mine, we must study our differences.

After settling in Arlington, Virginia, and starting our family, I learned of the founding of a new Mormon quarterly journal, the one I had volunteered for when it was just a gleam in the eye of my friend

Gene England. He and Wes Johnson, both doctoral candidates at Stanford, had gathered a group of former institute students to found an independent publication dedicated to the process of "bringing their faith into dialogue with human experience as a whole and fostering artistic and scholarly achievement based on their cultural heritage." I joined their editorial board.

Little did I know that ten years later, I would become editor of *Dialogue: A Journal of Mormon Thought,* moving it to Virginia where it would become a kind of cottage industry. With the office in the basement, I could run the house and the journal together. Volunteers and staff, which sometimes included my bishop husband and our three children, seemed to meld the five ideals of Lambda Delta Sigma and my professional and family life into one integral whole.

During the six and a half years of my editorship, I believed that *Dialogue* was acting in the volunteer tradition of church and community. We were in touch with some of the best minds and hearts in the church, who represented the examined life in an increasingly complicated and frightening world.

During this time, I was convinced more than ever that the doctrines and the beliefs of the church were strong enough to withstand analysis and discussion. I believed I was following the scriptural admonition that I should be anxiously engaged in a good cause, bringing to pass much that is good of my own free will.

### III

A few years ago, we in Zion East were heartened to learn of the brightly colored sandbags Salt Lakers had banked around their city during spring floods. A disastrous experience the year before had taught them to be prepared. It occurred to me that I need metaphorical sandbags to protect against the floods. Brother B. often talked of these, and he placed "creativity" at the top of his stack of sandbags, or near the top of his "pyramid of values."

"When we are creative, we are truly in the image of God," wrote Bennion. It is the creative self that provides the energy to write poetry, to paint pictures, and to learn a better way of living. In my own search for creativity, I try to excavate the submerged artifacts of my dreaming self. My diary, which I have kept off and on since the age of thirteen, records my dreams and my waking interpretations. This diary gives me inspiration and support for many ambitions. Getting to know myself in this way is the beginning of wisdom. But dreams remain insubstantial unless work can be found that meets the needs of the whole person. So I have learned that I must plan a day or a week that allows time for meditation, study, and prayer. I have aspired to be a writer, teacher, friend, mother. Since all of these jobs require me to reach for what I feel is beyond me, I need creativity and the courage to apply my inspiration. A truly creative person can seem threatening to other people, just as a new way of doing something makes them feel insecure. Sometimes members of the church react to a new idea as if it showed lack of faith. It takes courage to believe in oneself and one's idea. As I grow older, I wonder how many of my ideas I have submerged because of the fear of being misunderstood and mistrusted. I wonder how much self-censorship I have applied before really trying out my idea on the group.

"A saint is someone who is taking a risk," says Dian Saderup, essayist. This fits psychologist Abraham Maslow's definition of a "self-actualized human being," one who has the courage to step out of the protective coloration of comfortable retreats to push back the frontiers of the self. My husband, who walks with two braces and a cane, must constantly take thought of details that others take for granted. So small a thing as a square of cellophane on the floor can bring him down. Because of his constant courage, I have overcome many of my own fears and phobias and have avoided the temptation to pass them on to our children.

Pillars, pillows, bolsters, sandbags. I suppose it doesn't matter which term I use to describe my faith as long as it helps me to walk uprightly with my God in a world that emphasizes the things that matter most.

[1986]

# III
## Moving On

# THE DIARY CHAIN

Mother, you don't understand!" loosely translated, means "You were never my age!" Breathes there a mother who has not heard, with sinking heart, such words from a daughter suddenly transformed from laughing girl to sulking sphinx?

Oh, to produce authentic, incontrovertible proof that, yes indeed, Mother was once her daughter's age, with all its temptations, frustrations, fears—and joys.

Luckily my diary was at the ready, and fourteen-year-old Mary was able to reach across the years to fourteen-year-old Lorraine with these words:

> I write a diary in the hope that someday I will have a daughter of my own who will have to go through some of the same things I am now experiencing and even though most of these entries sound awfully silly and dumb, they have been and are me. They mark changes in me and show things I have learned. There's nothing extraordinary about me, nothing extraordinary happens to me, but to a teen-age girl, everything is new and different and perhaps some day these entries will help a teen-age girl of my own.

At that moment my relationship with my daughter turned toward maturity and friendship. Our problems did not immediately solve themselves through the sharing of the diary, but the many readings to follow triggered long-buried memories of mine and well-kept secrets of hers.

We began by comparing our backgrounds. Mine was a semi-rural life on an acre of orchard and garden in East Mill Creek, a suburb of the LDS church capital. I remember when the ice box was put out to pasture (literally deposited there) and the refrigerator installed. I remember when the wood stove gave way to the gas furnace. I remember the exciting moment when my brother's answer to a radio question won us a free demonstration of a new-fangled contraption called a television. All my school friends were Mormons, and my intimates were a band of cousins growing up within a six-block radius of my house. Some of the students in my high school were considered "fast," but "fast" meant a kiss on the first date, or maybe the second. My parents were distinctly shocked the first and only time I brought home a boy not of our religion.

Yes, mine was an insulated world, disturbed only by rumors of a conflict in Korea that finally drafted a few of my college friends. Born during the last gasp of the Great Depression, I recorded the end of World War II in my diary when I was fourteen years old.

Lorraine was born just before Vietnam, the civil rights marches, and the Kennedy and King assassinations. She grew up in a series of apartments and houses in Arlington, Virginia, a suburb of the nation's capital. She felt conspicuous in the ward because she was the bishop's daughter and conspicuous in school because she was a Mormon. Some of her wide circle of friends worried us because they sometimes drank and smoked pot. My husband taught me to drive a car when I was thirty-three; Lorraine learned at fifteen. I left Utah for the first time at sixteen on a trip to Wyoming; Lorraine by sixteen had made several cross-country trips and had traveled with us through Europe in a camper bus. When Lorraine left for college, she traveled 2,200 miles by plane; I had simply boarded the downtown bus. My serious traveling began after marriage; Lorraine participated in a BYU study abroad program and took a Caribbean cruise with us when she was twenty.

Lorraine and I tried to close the gaps between her experiences and mine by comparing descriptions of some of the important stations on our life journeys. First, we had to clear up some vocabulary problems in my diary. She asked me to define "wolf" as it applied to a boy; "het -up" as in "Mama got all het-up when I didn't get home from school on time"; "maul" as in "I don't like boys to try to maul me"; "hub-ba-hubba" as in "Hubba-hubba, is he ever handsome!"

Lorraine noticed right away the difference in our testimonies. At fourteen I wrote, "I am so in love with the church! I know as truly as if I had had a revelation that God made the LDS church and Joseph Smith did have a revelation. I know it with every part of me. I hope I can go to the celestial kingdom when I die." It was only after a great deal of soul-searching and testing that Lorraine was finally able to say, at age twenty-two, "I have finally understood what the concept 'keep the commandments and you will be happy' means. . . . I feel I am changing for the better—a spiritual rebirth, you might say."

My insulated upbringing had caused me to believe that people born into the church were just naturally born with a testimony. But, as I pointed out to Lorraine, my tests were waiting. It's just that I was a late bloomer.

We both began realizing that under our cultural differences were sibling heartbeats. "I have no freedom," I cried at fifteen. "I can never go shopping because I have no money and am hardly ever allowed to ride the bus. I have to wait until Dad remembers to give me a dollar. What's a girl going to do with a dollar? They don't realize that pretty new clothes are important to a girl's confidence. They don't understand me." And yet only a few pages later, after exulting in a new Easter dress, these words: "I am so thankful for the privilege of being me, of going through life with the things I was born with and the things I have the power to attain."

Our continuing involvement in the sagas of our diaries placed us on a local speaking circuit, where we became known informally as the Mother-Daughter-Diary-Duo—this during the years when the church was pushing personal history writing in Sunday School and Mutual. In her speech, Lorraine said that "Mother's descriptions have shown me she really can understand me. We have learned to understand each other." She went on to describe her own diary-keeping methods. "I started keeping a diary in the fourth grade. At first I wrote what Davis Bitton has called the 'I dug potatoes today diary': I woke up, I got out of bed, I went to school, and so on. This can be very boring. After a while I began writing about how I felt. Soon I found that my diary was not just a book, but a friend. It has helped me solve problems. It is a way to relieve tension. I can trust it to keep my secrets. It is fun to look back on, and I can read it aloud to those I love."

As she grew up, Lorraine often read back into her early life and would come to me exclaiming, "Mother! Listen to this! I can't believe I said this. I can't believe I felt this way!"

An important stage in our journey was reached in Lorraine's last year in high school when she had an important dream, triggered no doubt by her study of *Our Town* in English class. In her dream she had died and been allowed to return to our kitchen just long enough to place a gift for me on the table—her diaries. This gift symbolized the trust we had built, a trust we hoped would last beyond a lifetime.

Lorraine's was a stormy adolescence. As a young girl, she was a budding feminist, outspoken, honest. One night she led her Beehive class into the office of the bishop (her father) to confront him with these words, "The church is unfair to women, blacks, and Beehive girls." She had noticed that when the boys went on a field trip to the White House to study presidential politics, the girls stayed behind to hear a lesson on the fact that women are allowed only one temple marriage, while blacks were not allowed in the temple at all.

Later she shocked ward members when her father, with a few minutes to spare at the end of sacrament meeting, called her from the audience to "bear her testimony." Her response: "I will bear my testimony when I choose to do so—not because someone tells me to."

I should have assured those who congratulated me for rearing a chip off the old block that my diaries prove that at her age, I was always ready to speak whether or not I knew what I was saying. What her father and I failed to realize at the time and what her diaries could have shown is that teenage years are times of intense and idealistic religious fervor. Lorraine, because of her integrity and sensitivity, was not willing to express what she did not deeply feel. Through our increasing intimacy, I gradually came to understand her deepest anxiety, her need for faith. She also needed to understand her sexual self, her social self, her intellectual self. Perhaps her "spiritual rebirth" would help her to unite these selves.

Strangely enough, Lorraine's search prompted her to leave BYU after three years and settle at the University of Maryland, where her activity in the College Heights singles ward led her to tell her diary: "For the first time in my life I can honestly say that the gospel and the love of God and my family are far more important to me than anything else. I still love dance, school, and social life, but I am learning my priorities."

I confess I was surprised when she came to me and expressed her desire to serve a mission. I suppose I was thinking what a fine meal her earlier words would make, "I will go on a mission when I can baptize and not before." But I was worried about her. She was almost finished with her dance degree and was dancing in a company. Was it wise to stop now? Wasn't she too mature to work along with nineteen-year-old male missionaries? Would she become depressed without her physical fitness regime? And where in the world would they send her, with so many dangerous countries to choose from?

My anxieties lessened, however, when I realized that this decision was the natural outcome of her search—as well as the fulfillment of one of her mother's youthful dreams. My diary records that when I went to the bishop to ask for a mission call, I was refused on the grounds that I was still attractive enough for marriage. I could now rejoice at the change in attitude and policy that allowed my daughter to make a choice and act on it. Now she writes from the Philippines:

> I feel closer to God, I feel my inner core strengthening. I'm learning a lot and growing a lot. I like being busy and disciplined. Everything I do is worthwhile. We are always visiting and teaching and making people smile and laugh. We study the scriptures and the gospel two hours a day. I like that. We never waste a second. Although I miss watching football and eating pizza, sitting in a tree and reading, or just lying on the bed with the family and laughing, I know I will be able to do all that again. This experience comes only once in a lifetime.

Before she left, Lorraine exacted two promises from me—to work on my poetry and to exercise. She taught me her version of the twenty-minute workout and gave me a motivating lecture that she believed would help me regain some of the strength I had lost during a recent illness. She also taught me her motto—If you don't follow your dream, you die.

"Mother," she said, "it's one thing to try and fail. It's another to let your poetry molder away in the file drawer because you didn't have the courage to try."

While Lorraine prepared to leave on her mission, my mother departed for hers. Lavinia Mitchell Lythgoe died on January 6, 1984, at the age of seventy-eight. My father, my brothers, my sister, and I gathered to prepare for the funeral. While searching for her temple clothes, we discovered a cache of diaries. We knew that Mother had kept a diary—we had been allowed to read it from time to time—but we were surprised at the extent of the volumes dating back to her early teens and ending just a few months before her death.

Dennis and I read the 1928 diary aloud to our father and mined material for the talks we would give at her funeral. This was the year of their courtship.

As a young woman, Mother kept her diary in the "dug potatoes today" style, a few lines a day or every few days, until the gradual layering formed a surprisingly satisfying collection. The method I once criticized as lacking in originality clarifies the importance of the ordinary in a woman's life. My own method of writing fitfully at great length, followed by long droughts, disappoints by comparison.

Her cryptic lines, precious in their brevity, beckon to me: "At Sunday School we learned for a positive fact that Jesus Christ was sent to fill a divine mission." "She was painted up so terribly that it hurt my eyes to look at her." "I caught the new boy at the factory looking at me with such eyes!" Each Monday night, home evening, was captured in detail—the prayers, the readings, the songs like her father's solo, "Where the Silverish Colorado Winds Its Way." Visits from the "ward teachers" and the Relief Society teachers were welcomed. Movies, books, band concerts, parades, and rides in the amazing new automobile form a sizeable chunk of social history.

She was wonderfully consistent. Her later diaries record visits from church leaders, along with birthday parties, holiday celebrations, and other special events in the lives of her children, grandchildren, brothers, and sisters. During her last bedridden months, visits became more precious. One entry simply reads, "No one came today." Her handwriting, always firm, remained readable to the end.

Now I stand, newly orphaned, holding the artifacts of her life up to the light, hoping to catch the true image of my mother. I seek my mother and I long to meet her, unencumbered, as friend and sister. Her diaries and mine and Lorraine's are links among us. Each time we consider these links, we see new configurations. Some mysteries will be replaced by certainties, but most of them will remain as long as we can ask questions.

[1984]

# THE VEIL

Our family had finished the pre-service reception and Brother Holbrook, the funeral director, had just closed the doors to the Relief Society room. As Mother's surviving sisters and their families filed past the coffin for the last time, my own sister took my hand and whispered, "You have to be the one to veil her face, Mary." Startled, I remembered a scene from twenty years ago when I had joined my husband in bidding farewell to his aunt. We had watched while her eldest daughter placed a yellow rose in the stiffened hands and bent down to lay the temple veil over the beloved face. This was the only time I had seen this ritual.

My brother pronounced a prayer over the pink coffin that Dad, my brothers, my sister, and I had chosen a few days before. It turned out to be the least expensive choice and the one that "looked most like Mother" with its brocaded exterior and its rose-covered interior. We then had to decide whether to leave it open for viewing. When the Holbrook family reconstructed her cancer-ravaged face working from photographs and prothesis, Dad was satisfied, so the lid remained up, and her name went up too at the entrance to the mortuary on a small marquee: Lavinia Mitchell Lythgoe. A warm memory brushed my cheek when I first saw it—her name written on a slip of paper for an eight-year-old daughter to keep on her pillow while Mother vacationed for the first time since her marriage. She had aspired to be a painter and a writer. She enjoyed seeing her name in print.

At first I thought it would be excruciatingly difficult to stand beside that reconstructed face while the real one with its delicate, slightly tipped nose and pale skin-tones of a redhead looked out from a colored photograph near the guest book. But by the end of the evening, I was able to rest my hand casually on the satin rim of the coffin, even laughing as I reminisced with friends and relatives. The rest of my family seemed relaxed, too, certainly more so than when our ordeal began two days before.

Dennis had arrived from Boston and I from Virginia to stay with Dad and plan the services with Tom and Gaye, who lived in Salt Lake City. On the flight out, I had made up my mind to speak even though a nerve ailment had left me with a speech impediment. As eldest child, I challenged the others to do likewise. After some discussion, Tom decided to sing, Dennis to speak, and Gaye to pray. We also chose Rex Curtis, former bishop and husband to my mother's niece, to deliver one of his fatherly, comforting sermons. Ione Palfreyman, ward organist, was also chosen, and Gaye's husband Al would pronounce the invocation. During this time, we alternately laughed, argued, cried, and suffered from migraine. (We called it our "group migraine," a condition we inherited from Mother.) Later, while searching through his personal papers, Tom found a long-forgotten slip of paper on which Mother had dictated the very program we had just created.

We then spent the next few hours in a fruitless search for Mother's temple clothes. We did find my temple dress, the one in which I had taken out my own endowments twenty-six years before. "I wish I could lose enough weight to wear a dress like that," Mother had said at the time. It pleased me, then, to deliver this dress to the Holbrooks, even though it was now large enough to clothe two of Mother's wasted body.

Our search also uncovered the first of a collection of diaries beginning about 1918 and ending a few months before her death. The small red diary of 1928 recounted her courtship and engagement with Dad. As Dennis read it aloud, Dad exclaimed, "Land! Mother had all the men after her!" Her girlish accounts of her "beaus" followed by her head-over-heels response to Dad, delighted him. "As soon as she met you, Dad," Dennis told him, "she never could see anyone else."

The question in all our minds during this emotionally heightened and curiously mirthful period was "How will we get through the program without breaking down?" I believed that Tom's solo would be the most trying. Apparently he thought so too, because after the program went to the printer, he called to say that he had decided to "get it over with" and be first. Tom's baritone voice always carries such a wallop, even in less emotional times, that Dennis, Gaye, and I doubted our ability to follow him.

Tom was the one who watched with Dad during the day and the night of Mother's leaving. It was he who heard the doctor say, "Let her go. Your mother has chosen it." It was he who prayed her through her last agony, he who called the mortuary.

Dennis and I decided to type out our remarks and to practice them until we could read them aloud at least once without crying. I chose my words carefully, and although it is not my habit to speak from a prepared text, I felt the typed pages would give me courage.

In spite of our careful plans, I was unprepared for the moment in the Relief Society room when, leaning over the coffin, I heard myself whisper, "I'm sorry, Mother," and pulled the veil down.

When I heard Tom's voice soaring out over the chapel benches, I said to myself, "If Tom can sing, I can speak." Although my voice broke slightly at the end of my eulogy, I was able to fulfill the prophecy made by one of my friends, "You will be able to speak. The Holy Ghost has promised to be with those who mourn."

I spoke of Mother's inherent joyousness as expressed in her diary; "My birthday! Oh, how wonderful to be alive!" and "Glorious Christmas day! We awoke and found Santa Claus had been." When, as a child, I learned that she and Dad were responsible for all the miraculous gifts, she swore me to secrecy and inducted me into the Santa Claus Club. "Santa Claus is real. He lives in the hearts of those who continue to believe in giving." Santa Claus was a symbol of her delight in all special occasions, in holidays, in visits from friends, relatives, home teachers, and visiting teachers. These visits were faithfully recorded throughout her diaries, along with the lonely line, in late 1979, "No one came today."

My remarks centered around Mother's search for her mission in life. She had said to me only two years before, "I know I was spared for some mission," and then, after a wistful pause, "The trouble is I don't know what that is yet." After puzzling for some time over this remarkable admission, I wondered if Mother had been suffering from the same seething ambitions that had always informed my own life. I was more puzzled when Gaye told me that Mother's last words to her were, "My mission is now over." Had she reviewed her own accomplishments and found them good?

Dennis also read from her diary, "Leo and I rode up Parley's Canyon and stopped and talked for a long time. Oh, wonderful! Wonderful! I became engaged!" Then much later, after Dad's cataract operation, "It was so good to have him home again. I missed him so much. I love him so much and after forty-seven and a half years of married life!"

Rex Curtis was satisfying in his evocation of Mother's devotion to her family and her church, and Gaye's and Al's simple prayers made us feel that we all had portrayed Mother at her best.

Of course, some of the most burning questions remained unanswered, even unasked. Why had she allowed her beautiful face to be eaten away by skin cancer, an ailment that in its early stages could have been easily cured? During that fifteen-year ordeal, our family had fasted, prayed, remonstrated, and argued until Dad had finally forbidden any more discussion. We watched as she took to her bed in a darkened room, unwilling to look at herself or others, behind a growth the size of a gas mask. It was then that Dennis sent a letter to President Spencer W. Kimball asking for advice. President Kimball's phone call to my mother began a chain of events that finally brought her to the care of a specialist who understood that "your little mother has been afraid of doctors all her life."

He was right, of course. But I knew the reason was more complicated than that. I knew it could be traced to her ill health as a child when another doctor had advised her mother, "Enjoy her while you can. She won't live long enough for you to raise her." Her survival led to a consuming interest in health and illness, to long hours in "health lectures" and much reading in a stack of books dedicated to cures most medical experts would call "quack." I saw that she might even have become a doctor herself.

During the years when the "sore" was growing, I felt personally responsible. As her eldest child, I was sure I could persuade her to seek help. A three-day family fast finally gave me permission to relinquish my burden. I understood that, as long as Mother had her wits, she also had the right to choose. The life extension finally granted her may have been the gift that allowed her to declare, "I was saved for some mission."

When the sun burst out over her gravesite during our last prayer that dark January day, we felt satisfied and we felt that she was satisfied.

After being fed by the Relief Society in the cultural hall at the ward, we went home with Dad to help him prepare for his time alone.

Two days later, at a luncheon with a few women friends, I found myself describing the veiling ceremony. Afterwards, I chided myself for voicing such an intimate experience; and over the next week, its image kept intruding on my thoughts as I was cleaning, organizing, and helping Dad with his finances. Dad, Dennis, Tom, Gaye, and I pored over photograph albums Mother had kept for so many years, exclaiming over the hodgepodge collection. Childhood pictures were crowded against recent ones with no particular plan. Who was that handsome man with the mutton chops? That lovely lady in the mutton sleeves? Why had Mother kept that unflattering picture of me as a fat teenager, along with an old photo of a boyfriend I can no longer call to mind? It was a treasure hunt and a guessing game.

From albums we moved to drawers, chests, boxes under beds. My old cedar chest, where I had stored my wedding dress, was now filled with yarn and dolls, mine and Gaye's. Other chests held my red-lace prom dress, tatting and crocheting from my grandmother's day, and a wooden pencil box given to me in the first grade as an inheritance. All through the house were boxes filled with letters and junk mail, jewelry, and notebooks. We zipped back and forth in time as if on a crazy amusement ride, sorting, categorizing, seeking significance. Mother's lifelong habit of never throwing anything away, which had always irritated me, now seemed a blessing. Most of the treasures of our childhoods were still in the house along with the artifacts of her own life that would help us to know her better.

I remember a passage from Eudora Welty's *A Writer's Beginnings*: "It seems to me, writing of my parents now in my seventies, that I see continuities in their lives that weren't visible to me when they were living."

I was sleeping in my mother's room. As I lay in her bed asking myself why she had chosen to die in such a narrow, uncomfortable berth, I gazed at her walls. A picture of me in wedding finery, a painting of the Great Salt Lake painted by Mother for my wedding present, a watch I had given her for her fiftieth wedding anniversary. As I gazed at these and other keepsakes, the image of the veiling continued to hang over my spirit. I had always believed the veiling of a woman's face to be an insult. And yet other more cheerful images came—a doll being lifted through a veil of tissue paper from a large box, and later, a smooth floral box of long-stemmed roses protected by a veil of moist, white paper. How sweet the smell! How romantic the promise! Remembering them only deepened the sting I was feeling.

A few days later, after going home to Virginia, I tried to write in my diary. But I found myself stopping at the moment of the veiling. For several days I tried to write and could not. Then one day I received a note from Maureen Ursenbach Beecher, who had been at the luncheon. "I treasure your sharing the moment of the veiling of your mother's face," she wrote. "I would not have thought of that part of our ritual until it came to me, so I appreciate knowing in advance. I kept hearing the Bach music of a similarly beautiful, painful moment: 'Es druckten deine lieben Haende / Mir die getreuen Augen zu'—the idea that one might go in peace if it were the loved one's loving hands which pressed the eyelids shut. That office in our family will be my sister's by seniority and proximity, but it pleases me to know that it will be lovingly done. For moments of anticipated tenderness, Mary, much thanks."

At that moment my veil of confusion lifted, as if Maureen had taken my experience and edited it for me. I knew that when Mother had finally worn out her body and could no longer "face" the loss of her face, she had chosen to give up the struggle, allowing her body to be laid away like an antique doll, now too fragile to be disturbed.

I think of another statement of Welty's: "Writing fiction has developed in me an abiding respect for the unknown in a human lifetime and a sense of where to look for threads, how to follow, how to connect, find in the thick of the tangle what clear line persists. The strands are all there: to the memory nothing is ever really lost."

So I honor what is unknown about my mother—the essential mystery of her being. I close the lid, and I am thankful.

[1984]

# GENTLE DAD

*"The ground must be cleared . . . you must tear down all the old out-buildings, for instance, which are worthless, and cut down the old cherry orchard."*—Lopakhin, in Chekhov's The Cherry Orchard

The phone rang at midnight. I groped it sleepily to my ear. It was my father's high priest group leader calling from Utah. "We are here in ward council meeting," he said. "We've just arranged to have your father's orchard bulldozed." I sat up, wide awake now. "The whole orchard? Isn't that a bit severe?" He agreed that it probably was, but my dad had given them orders to take the whole thing. The ward leaders had declared a "Leo Lythgoe Day" and were hiring equipment to help clear the orchard and the garden in a general cleanup. It had suddenly occurred to them that "Mary and Dennis might not like it."

I told him that I would prefer to save the live trees and that I would talk to Dennis in Boston and to Tom and Gaye in Salt Lake.

Then I stood up and started pacing. Vivid pictures flooded my mind: Me as a child in the cherry trees, me picking pears and apples from the lower branches while Dad picked from the higher ones. Warm and juicy apricots and plums. And alfalfa feathering my legs as I ran through the fields and up to the irrigation ditch to dip my feet in the water and smell the fresh mint.

I cried. I even went to the bookshelf and took down Chekhov's *The Cherry Orchard*. Lamenting the loss of the family orchard, one of the characters says, "Oh, my childhood, my innocence! I used to sleep in this nursery, I looked out into the orchard, happiness awoke with me each morning." Gayev says, "Yes, and the orchard will be sold for our debts." And Lyubov Anreyevna adds, "Look, our dead mother walks in the orchard . . . in a white dress!"

The play ends on "a distant sound" that seems to come from the sky, the sound of a "snapped string mournfully dying away. A stillness falls, and nothing is heard but the thud of the ax on a tree far away in the orchard."

At daylight, I called Tom in Salt Lake City. I told him that when Dad's bishop had offered to help clear the orchard of dead trees, limbs, and weeds, Dad had said, "You may as well take all the trees."

"Trees keep the air fresh," I said, "and they keep the land from turning to dust and blowing away. Dennis and I would hate to go to Utah to find that our family homestead had become the little house on the prairie."

Tom promised to save the trees.

Dad had planted the trees nearly fifty-five years ago after moving into the house he had built for his bride—my mother. He had worked hard to keep the trees producing, and he had taught his children to pick. The cherries had to keep their stems as they dropped into the bucket, the pears had to be yellow but not too soft, the apples burnished with gold or red, depending on their family name. Astrachan, Jonathan, Delicious—how the names make my mouth water!

In summer and early fall, we used to help sell the fruit, lining it up in bushel baskets in front of the house. As soon as prospective buyers pulled up, I would call for Mother to make the transactions. I was not good at making change.

In an oral history interview, Dad recorded that in good years our acre yielded more than 250 bushels of fruit. We also sold Mother's private crop, raspberries. Every July, Mother would suit up for the assault on the tender berry among the thorns—long stockings, hat, sunglasses, even stockings on the arms. Occasionally, she would draft me as helper. If keeping stems on the cherries was a trick, gently detaching the ripe raspberry from its convex holder required a dexterity it would take me years to develop. Of course, if the berry wasn't ripe enough, it wouldn't come. If we should be clumsy enough to disturb it before its time, it could be lost. Mother had just the right, light touch, as she did at almost everything she put her hand to.

Dad, however, did not have the light touch when it came to the pruning of trees. One year, he lopped off one-half of the perfect "v" from one of two Paradise trees in our front yard, leaving a gnarled wound where a backrest had been. After he chopped down the cherry trees, I asked him whether he had discovered buried treasure. "What treasure?" he asked.

"Ruth and I buried a tin can with some letters in it that we weren't supposed to dig up until the trees were cut down or until we married, whichever came first." (Ruth was my mother's youngest sister, only four years older than I.) No, he hadn't found our treasure. "What did the letters say?"

"They were prophecies. Mine said Ruth would marry Tom Challis and Ruth's said I would marry Kenneth Huffman." I was proven right, Ruth wrong.

I asked Dad why the trees couldn't have remained standing as a kind of monument to my childhood. My favorite Bing cherry tree had a strong limb for chinning and a perfect seat for me to hide in with my books. It was my fantasy tree. I was Tarzana of the Apes, Wonder Woman, and Anne of Green Gables. My tastes were nothing if not eclectic.

After all, I told Dad, the trees weren't in anyone's way; in fact, they stood as a protective fence between us and the world to the north. Dad replied that dead trees were a menace and an eyesore.

He also had a penchant for spraying the trees with arsenic. Mother finally won out on that, though, and he stopped. From then on, the fruit was small but still juicy and plentiful.

It always seemed to me that his practical attitude toward trees didn't mesh with his soft heart. We could always tell where he was sitting in church because he would loudly clear his throat when he was trying to control his tears. Any scripture, testimony, or musical solo could bring them on. If one of us should be on the program, we could count on his sniffling throughout.

Mother used to send me to the orchard for a "willow," which she would then use to switch my legs. Dad could usually discipline us without such props, but he reminded us that Mother was the one who was stuck with "raising" us during the years when he worked two jobs.

He must have spent quality time with us because I vividly recall his stories, his night nursing during flu season, his companionship in the orchard, his willingness to lend an ear to our complaints. He had an imaginative way of calling us out of nightmares. Sitting on the edge of my bed, he fed me segments of oranges until my blood sugar reached a high enough level to chase the goblins away.

Why then was he so hard on the trees? That question puzzled me so much when I was young that I penned a poem called "Dad So Gentle":

> Dad sang in the morning / As he called us from sleep / But he sometimes wore overalls / White with the spray of death / Dad in his reading voice / Hesitated over our stories at night / And by day his shears / Crippled the Paradise trees.

I never showed this poem to him. And I forgot about it until the time came for clearing the orchard.

Tom reported that Dad had watched the path of the bulldozer with sadness and some agitation. He seemed glad to have the work done, but sorry too. When I visited him a few months later, I walked around what was left of the orchard and the garden. The logs from the trees were piled behind the garage and the raspberries were gone. Recent rains had turned the ground to mud. A stand each of apple and pear trees guarded the house on either side.

I paced around the remains of the barn remembering Buttercup and Daisy, our two milk cows. Dad had tried to teach me to milk, with indifferent success. I loved to watch him milk, though, pulling from his three-legged stool as foam gathered on the rim of the bucket. He carries the milk to the kitchen where he strains it through cheesecloth. In winter, Mother sets the milk in pans on the front porch. After the cream rose to the top, often with a thin coating of ice, Mother churned butter and created one of my favorite elixirs—fresh buttermilk. She stored the milk, the buttermilk, and the cream in the old ice box on the back porch.

In his oral history, Dad says that during his first ten years on the railroad, the two cows gave enough milk for him to sell twenty pints a day to his fellow workers and several quarts to the neighbors.

Of course, the cows had to be fed, so in summer Dad rented a team of horses and a hayrack so my brothers and I could stomp the hay down after Dad forked it up to us. Sinking into the prickly cloud, we rode it home where we stomped it again while he arranged it in a stack near the barn.

So many memories of the orchard and the barn! My childhood, beginning in the Depression, spanned a transition period called by some writers, "The Great Leap." I remember when we changed from coal to gas, when the cookstove in the kitchen and the heating stove in the living room were torn out to make way for the electric stove, the refrigerator, and the furnace. I remember when the county sewer finally snaked its way through our neighborhood, replacing the cesspool.

After I had finished my weepy walk through the mud and weeds of the denuded orchard, I had time to notice how very tired Dad seemed. He kept sighing, "It's a heck of a note. Getting old." I reasoned that he probably hadn't eaten lately. I knew he had given up fixing food for himself except for an occasional can of soup or a frozen chicken pie. Tom and Gaye often brought food, and we had convinced the ward food brigade that instead of casseroles, a plate of food from their own dinners would be best. Dad didn't seem to know what to do with leftovers except feed them to the chickens.

Before Mother's death, he looked so tired that we almost believed Mother when she said, "Dad and I are going to die together." But after his long service as Mother's nurse ended, restful nights and outdoor chores seemed to strengthen him for a while. But now he seemed distant and distracted.

He reported hearing Mother's voice calling in the night and the ringing of early morning doorbells.

On my visits, I noticed that, during the first few hours, he appeared pessimistic and sad; but after a few days, his spirits would rise. He and I watched television together, and his sense of humor improved noticeably. I thought I knew what he needed—company. Sitting alone most of every day was giving him too much time to brood.

"Dad, why don't you come and visit me in Washington? We could have someone watch this house. I have a nice room on the ground floor with a television and everything you need." He refused, as I knew he would, but I continued to hope that one day he would visit me, and then if all went well, he might want to move in.

Meanwhile, I urged him to talk about his early years in Cowley, Wyoming, that small town that was part of what church historians call "The Last Colony." My grandfather, Thomas Lythgoe, was one of the first pioneers to build a house in that barren frontier—a log cabin as rustic as any in the Old West. A picture of it, with my dad's family in front, had appeared in *The Improvement Era* many years ago. When Mormons talk about their four-generation pioneer heritage, I can say, "I don't have to go back any further than my grandfather."

Having already settled on a fertile dairy farm in Granger, Utah, Grandfather uprooted his family. Dad, the eldest, was four years old. This was in 1900, when the Brigham Young style of settling impossible areas was supposedly over. Cowley historian Mark Partridge claims that the many converts arriving in Utah from foreign lands forced the church to look for suitable "arable" land in neighboring states.

I am puzzled at this explanation. Surely Utah's population was still sparse enough in 1900 for people like my grandfather to stay put. The method they used to locate land puzzles me even more. In the dead of winter, a party of thirteen men was dispatched to Idaho, Montana, and Wyoming. With Apostle Abraham O. Woodruff at the head, they arrived at Eagle's Nest, Wyoming, where they met with William Cody, "Buffalo Bill." He hinted that the Mormons could share his permit to construct an irrigation system through a large part of the "Stinking Water" area, or the Shoshone River Valley near a small branch of the church in Burlington. With that, the party returned to Utah and recommended that President Lorenzo Snow call a few hundred families to the Big Horn.

My grandmother's brother, George Harston, was in the first company of covered wagons. He pitched a tent on the salt sage flats near the river and sent for his wife and family, his brother, Will Harston, his sister, Mary Harston Lythgoe, and their families. They left fertile dairy farms in East Mill Creek and Granger for a land that would be without water until a canal more than thirty miles long could be constructed. Partridge reports that "there is no evidence that any samples of the soil were taken" before the pioneers were called. He admits that since the exploring party spent only two days on the proposed project, the "investigation could not have been very thorough."

"Why do you think they went?" I asked Dad.

"I don't know. It sure was a mistake."

I was taken aback by that answer. Having listened to Dad's colorful stories about the characters in his hometown, I had always believed that Dad was cherishing a rosy picture of life in the ranchlands not far from the beautiful Big Horn Mountains. When I was sixteen, Dad had taken Tom and me to Wyoming on the train. It was a grand adventure for me, my first trip out of Utah. We stayed with Uncle Will, where I promptly fell in love with his twenty-year-old son, my cousin Garner. I tried to drive a tractor, tried to ride a horse, watched the irrigation process over a vast terrain, visited the dry lake where couples liked to "spoon," and took a trip to Montana to check fences on another Harston ranch. I formed a lasting attachment to the scenery.

My diary records that in Cowley I felt free: "In Salt Lake there are too many houses, trees and mountains hemming me in." Since none of our relatives approved of my cousin-love, I vowed to remain single until such time as I could find another dark-haired, green-eyed, open-hearted young man like Garner. I mourned the end of my visit to Cowley: "That happy week is gone-gone-gone! What will I do? Garner is my standard for a husband. If I can't have him, I want someone with those same wonderful qualities." Not surprisingly, my choice of husband—ten years later—turned out to be a young man very much like my cousin.

Anyway, it came as a shock to discover that, although Dad could discourse lovingly on life in Cowley, he was no more romantic about it than he was about dead trees.

My father blamed Uncle George for the trek to Cowley. "He was a pioneer! He drove a team from here clear out there. Swimming across rivers and everything else!" According to Dad, the pioneer spirit meant that Uncle George "always had to be going somewhere! He couldn't stay in one place."

I remembered Uncle George as an old man with white hair and pink skin who used to stay with us in the summers. He had a cleanliness fetish and could be heard washing, washing his already transparent skin, over and over in the night, like Lady Macbeth. One summer, the pit underneath the back lawn had to be dug all over again. Though no one blamed Uncle George aloud, it was understood that he was the one who finally flooded the cesspool.

We were fond of Uncle George, though, partly because of Dad's adventure on the ice. One night when the motherless boy, my father, was out "huntin' Pa," he found him with Uncle George sawing ice on the Sage Creek Reservoir. When Dad started across and fell in, Uncle George pulled him out by the shirt collar. "Pa wrapped me in a blanket, and we got on Old Pint and away we went home. Uncle George was always kidding me about trying to walk on the water!"

It was sad that this hardy pioneer spent his last years wandering up and down the West Coast and the Intermountain West, finally dying alone in a motel. He had left Cowley for another farming adventure in Idaho where his wife died and left him alone. He started wandering, finally taking a job in California. We were given to understand that his last visit to Cowley had brought on a depression that never left him. It seems that everything had changed direction. His former house was on the wrong side of the street. The town he had helped build from scratch was no longer home to him. The sun rose in the west and settled in the east. As a basically directionless person myself, I think I understood Uncle George's despair.

As I questioned Dad further, I realized that neither he nor I knew much about my namesake, my grandmother. She had died in child-birth, leaving my grandfather with five children, two sons and three daughters, Dad being the eldest. The brief entry in Partridge's account describes her as a woman whose house and children were always "neat and clean." Other family members have declared that she possessed a beautiful singing voice. At her death, her other children went to live with Uncle George's family, leaving Dad alone with his father. Using an injured foot as an excuse, Dad dropped out of school. His father said, "If you're not gonna go to school, you're gonna work!" As co-owner of Cowley's first threshing machine, he put Dad to work "cutting bands on the thresher from early morning until late at night."

I pictured the thirteen-year-old going home alone to the little log house. "Land, it was darker than a stack of black cats in that town— there were no lights, you know. Pa wasn't home and I'd go climb into bed scared to death. Sometimes I'd get a horse and go huntin' Pa all over town." So, while alone with his son, Grandpa decided to give him the gift of work. "Whatever job I could do, I worked hard at. And I gave all the money I earned to Pa."

I tried to remember what Grandpa Lythgoe was like. Uncle Billy, Dad's half-brother, describes him as a "real cowboy." At the age of eighty-six he could leap on a horse bareback and rein in a herd of runaway cattle. Lean, wiry, tough, he was also a deeply caring person.

Uncle Billy told this experience. "I was fifteen and worried about the big questions of life and death. I finally screwed up my courage. I asked Pa what he thought death was. He didn't hesitate. He said, 'Death is the greatest adventure in life.' When he came to his last illness, he called me in and told me that he didn't want to be given drugs that would knock him out. 'I want to be there when I die!'"

When Dad was twenty years old, his father married Rosetta King Black, Cowley's first schoolteacher and a widow with six children to add to Tom Lythgoe's five. Shortly after the Lythgoe family moved to the Black farm, Dad tried to enlist in the navy. He was rejected because of flat feet. Then in one of the many ironies of his life, he was accepted into the army infantry, where he walked on his flat feet through training periods in Utah, New Mexico, and New Jersey, then to the front lines in France, arriving a few days after the armistice. He survived the flu epidemic of 1918, during which his fellow soldiers "dropped like flies" around him.

At twenty-six, he was asked to serve a mission for the church. "Did you want to go?" Dennis asked him. "Land, no! I didn't know why the heck they wanted to send me. They just kept after me until they talked me into it. I said I would go as long as they wouldn't make me talk at the Farewell." He was called to the California mission, where he spent most of his time in Nevada—Elko, Reno, Susanville, Tonipah. He claimed he was not a good missionary: "I was no preacher!"

When he was released, Dad did not return to Cowley, but to Salt Lake City where he had inherited some land from his mother. In fact, the trip Tom and I took with him was his first trip back since his mission, almost twenty-two years before. And he worried all the way there about the possibility of being asked to deliver a missionary "homecoming speech."

In Salt Lake City, he found a job as a blacksmith helper on the Denver and Rio Grande railroad and married another California missionary—Agnes Anderson from Ephraim, Utah, who died ten months later in childbirth. It was 1930 and four years later when he married my mother, Lavinia Mitchell, and settled on his land in a new frame house. "We were sitting out there almost all alone." One of his sisters lived next door, and there was one other house farther down Twentieth East. "We could see through the poplar trees across the street almost down to Highland Drive two miles away."

Listening to Dad and re-reading his oral history interview, I realized that his buoyant spirit and sense of humor had kept me from noticing the hardships of his life.

Unemployed for two years during the Great Depression, he had almost lost the house. After that, he worked two shifts a day at the railroad. To the question, "Did you have to work that hard?" he answered, "I thought I did!" When diesel engines replaced his labor, he went to work for a neighbor who had constructed new houses on the east bench of the Wasatch Mountains, near East Mill Creek. His job was to superintend the private water system that serviced the homes. Beginning with two pumps, the system expanded as more houses were built. He had to hook them up to the meters, fix any leaks, and keep the pressure up in a system of pumps and boosters that, after his retirement, was sold to the city.

He liked the work. "It kept me interested. I liked it a lot better than the railroad, and I made more money. It kept me thinking. At night I had to regulate it so that in the morning I'd have all the tanks full. If I didn't have the tanks full in the morning, they'd be out of water before night."

His duties—keeping the tanks full in the morning so they wouldn't go dry at night—became a symbol for me. In the mornings he came in and closed my bedroom windows, singing, "Oh, it's great to get up in the morning, in the good old summertime." Though I tend to be a night person, I formed a desire to be like him—to welcome each day and to put in a full day's work on whatever I chose to do.

As his ninetieth birthday approached, we children decided to celebrate. Dennis, whose youngest son had never met his grandfather, decided to take his whole family out to Salt Lake from Boston for the occasion. When Dennis called to tell him, Dad said, "I may not be here." Dennis laughed and assured Dad that we would all be there.

I arrived a week early and stayed with Dad. Dennis, his wife Marti, and their children were with her parents a few blocks away. Tom and Gaye were busy planning the party that we had decided to keep secret from Dad until the last minute. A similar plan for our parents' fiftieth wedding anniversary had worked out beautifully.

Dad had been sharing his dreams with me, dreams in which he heard Mother calling him, but when he gets out of bed to go to her, he meets only the lonely silence. He admitted that he had fallen in his bedroom a few times. I began to feel uneasy about plans for the party. Suppose he's not up to it?

A few nights later, I took my laundry to the washing machine in the basement before leaving for a meeting. Since I knew Dad had stopped going down the basement stairs, I instructed him not to worry about my laundry—I would soon be back. An hour later, I was called to the phone: "Your father is in the hospital." Dennis had found him unconscious on the floor in the basement next to my laundry. His head had dented the water heater and bled on the cement floor.

By the time I arrived, Tom, Dennis, and the bishop had administered to him; and the attending physician at the emergency room had decided that the blow on the head had resulted from a heart attack, and not the other way around. Attempts to revive him failed. We stood around his body as it lay covered with a sheet on the table. Al Johnson, Gaye's husband, said a prayer.

Instead of a birthday party we planned a funeral.

A few days later, as I looked out the kitchen windows at the pear and apple trees on the south side of the orchard, I was happy that they were still standing, still changing color.

On the morning of the funeral, I looked out just in time to see a rainbow-striped, hot-air balloon as it floated past the trees and disappeared somewhere in the direction of the lake. I took that as a sign that Dad's buoyancy was still a force in the universe.

Rex Curtis, our cousin and one of Mother's funeral speakers, told us that he believed the spirits of the dead hover over us until after the burial. That was a comfort, but it did not keep me from waking in the night and worrying about my part in his death. He should have died quietly in his sleep when we were still here to keep him company or he should have died while telling one of his Cowley stories. Instead, he died trying to serve me—so like him!—when I should have been serving him.

Finally, one morning I awoke with the awareness of a particularly vivid dream. In the dream, Dad is living in my home in Virginia. He approaches me as I prepare to serve breakfast, puts his arms around me, and whispers, "Mary, I love you." Then he sits down at the table and quietly dies.

Obviously, the dream had restaged his death according to my needs. I could see that the dream was also telling me that I was making progress in my mourning labor—that I was learning to forgive myself. I already knew that Dad had forgiven me.

Now my regrets center around wasted time. Why hadn't I spent more time documenting his life? Dad was such a good storyteller. Why hadn't I been less selfish, more attuned to his needs, to the rhythm of his life?

I wish I had asked the same questions Uncle Billy had asked his father. How did Dad feel about death? Was he getting ready for it and would he welcome a chance to talk about it?

At least, I think I now understand his attitude about the trees that were no longer producing enough to pay for the space they occupied. He believed in giving a full day's work in return for his own space. No longer able to care for the aging orchard, he no longer wished to look at the neglected trees nor to sit alone in his life.

[1986]

# SURPRISE PARTY:
# MEDITATIONS ON AGING

*"Inside this stupid old body, I'm still young!"*—Mary Carson, *in the movie,* The Thorn Birds

## I

I don't recall the exact moment that age caught up with me. I think it was shortly after the Big Five-O, a few days after my birthday surprise party thrown by the *Dialogue* staff. I have had many surprise parties in my life, but this time I was really surprised.

It was Thursday, *Dialogue*'s weekly volunteer night. I was miffed because the staff seemed loath to ready a large subscription mailing. Finally the group shouted "Surprise!" and unmasked a cake topped with the *Dialogue* logo. The cake was amazing and so were the gifts.

In the midst of friends and co-workers, I knew I was the same kid who had enjoyed her first surprise party on her fifth birthday, and I have never stopped being surprised. Having long believed that the ability to be surprised would keep me young, I hadn't counted on being surprised by the face in the mirror. It is no longer young, and what's more, nobody tells me any more that it is.

I grew up looking young for my age. I inherited this from my parents. Mother's age was usually guessed at a decade younger. For most of her life, she had a peaches and cream complexion with no wrinkles. Dad's face was smooth and ruddy until he died, just before his ninetieth birthday.

At sixteen, I looked thirteen; at twenty-one I was asked for my work permit. When I was twenty-three and visiting Las Vegas for the first time, I was refused entrance to the casinos. Only a few years after my marriage, I was being taken for Chick's daughter by folk who assumed his fashionable black and white locks meant old age.

I was always admonished, good naturedly, that I would appreciate this youthful look when I finally did grow old. Well, I guess I am old now, because I would appreciate it if someone would mistake me for a younger woman.

Perhaps my old age was brought on by letting my hair go gray. When Chick had the gray hair and I the tinted locks, I was young. Does this mean that old age is simply a matter of appearance? Should I care if people can't see the young girl who is still in there kicking?

The worst part is that I have lost the beauty I didn't know I had. Oh, I was no beauty queen, but I must have been pleasing enough, and if pictures of me—even five years ago—are any indication, there have been long stretches when I wasn't even fat.

A perusal of photo albums reveals that I put on some "baby fat" at thirteen or so, took it off at fifteen or so, and was not overweight enough to matter until my first pregnancy. Since then, I have been genuinely fat several times, but never the sweaty, puffy-faced junior blimp I am now!

Yet I do not yearn to go back. For instance, I wouldn't want to be twenty-five again. Not that I wasn't happy at twenty-five, but I am enjoying life so much more now. That is, I have learned to appreciate life and cope with most of my phobias.

Thirty-five was good. This was probably because I was acting out my mother's belief that "thirty-five was the very best age to be." At thirty-five, our children had been born and were doing well, *Dialogue* had just been founded, and I was emerging from the heat of the kitchen and looking out at the world again.

Forty-five was good too. I had a job I loved, the children had grown into my wonderful friends, and everybody said I didn't look a day over thirty-five.

But now I am fifty-five. Some of my friends say they like my naturally "frosted" locks—they call them "cute"—and others appear shocked. "I thought you were blonde!" they croak. "Wasn't everybody?" I retort.

I am thinking of tinting my hair again—to a nice "bread and butter blonde." Some crime news made me think of it. It seems, elderly, gray-haired women were being hoodwinked by a good Samaritan driver who flagged them down, convinced them their wheels were about to roll off, and stole their cars from under their trusting, aging noses.

I don't really know what age I am inside, but I do know that the child in me is still alive. It is that child who can still wonder and be surprised.

## II

*Move to the front / of the line / a voice says, and suddenly / there is nobody / left standing between you / and the world, to take / the first blows / on their shoulders . . .—Linda Pastan, "The Death of a Parent"*

At an Exponent Day dinner, Emma Lou Thayne announced she had reached the Big Five-O and was now "the world's oldest orphan." She was standing with the wide-open eyes of the poet at a path suddenly lonely, with no one up ahead to call out warnings.

At the time I felt smug. My parents were still alive, and what's more, I was younger than Emma Lou. Now my parents have gone on ahead, and I realize that I, too, am teeming with questions I wish I had asked them. I now look to other mentors and friends.

Two of these, Virginia Sorensen Waugh and Esther Eggertsen Peterson, have imprinted themselves on my psyche. Virginia, Mormon novelist and subject of my master's thesis, survived the loss of her second husband and is now, at age seventy-five, living near her children and grandchildren in North Carolina. I have visited her on her "hill" in her little house overlooking a pond and a meadow complete with horses and cows. She calls me her "Boz" and "one of the young ones," and discourses on the joys that still await me. She wastes little time lamenting the past nor regretting lost opportunity. She sorts the artifacts of her life, ponders her next book, but is in no hurry.

Even though she is widowed and in her eighty-first year, Esther is still fighting for consumer rights in third-world countries. I often think of Virginia and Esther in the same breath because they are cousins, both from Utah, good friends to each other and to me. Lately I think of them as the two sides of my own personality—Virginia, the introspective novelist, and Esther, the extrovert and activist.

I am constantly refreshed by those minds that have not aged. I could name dozens of them. This makes me believe that it is not so much age but the use of time that is important.

Henry Adams once made a provocative statement about old age. "One has only to be old enough in order to be as young as one will." Perhaps he meant that the old have cut away the excesses from life and have stopped caring about the unimportant. In this way, each new day is an adventure.

## III

*Let death be by surprise . . .—Line from a poem I've forgotten*

Because my father was the oldest person I have known, I am studying his path to old age.

Son of a hardscrabble pioneer from the Big Horn Basin in Wyoming, he was motherless at thirteen and he quit school to work for his father and other struggling farmers in the area. Later, after a stint in the infantry, he served a mission for the church in Nevada. Both experiences were frustrating. In the army he was trained and sent to France, where he was marched to the front just in time for the armistice. His mission was held together by baling wire and his scant savings. He baptized only one eight-year-old and spent long hours hitchhiking in the desert.

He returned, not to Cowley, but to Salt Lake City and the land his mother left him. By the time he met my mother, he had buried his first wife and stillborn child. At thirty-four, he had learned to be alone and to love hard work.

I could attribute Dad's longevity to heredity, hard work, and as he put it, "Mother's cooking," but mostly I think his old age took him by surprise. In his last years, he served his invalid wife so completely that we were sure she would outlive him. But she went first, and he soon decided that life without work was intolerable.

When we gathered for his ninetieth birthday, we didn't tell him about the party being planned for him at the church. A surprise would be better, we thought. But he was the one who surprised us. Three days before his birthday, he died, and we planned a funeral instead.

Now it seems fortuitous that he was able to choose to go. "I may not be here," he had said. Unlike Dylan Thomas, who advised his father to rant and rave against the dying of the light, I can say that my father did go "gentle into that good night." Though his old age may have surprised him, he was ready for the next step.

I could ask for no better model.

[1986]

# THE WALKING CURE

One misty, moisty morning in mid-February 1978, I awoke, stared out the window at the gray world, and said to myself, "I am going to die." Now, I knew that I probably wouldn't drop dead at that moment, or even that day, but as I reviewed all the semi-challenging events planned for the next year or two, I knew that I was not equal to the task. Outings that I should be anticipating with joy—like meeting our missionary son in Spain—gave me the urge to lie down with a cold compress on my brow. Layers of symptoms wrapped themselves around my mostly supine body like a cocoon of fiberfill that I was unable to shed. Chronic ailments I had lived with off and on for years seemed to have taken permanent lodgings in my body—migraine, insomnia, the heartbreak of psoriasis, overweight—and added goodies, like numb fingers and an inability to bend my head forward without experiencing shooting pains in arms and legs. And worst of all, a constant, low-level depression that aggravated all my phobias. I won't go into those except to say that I was becoming more and more agoraphobic. I was staying more and more at home, loath to brave the beltway or even my neighborhood.

Of course, I had visited the trusted family doctor for a checkup. In a brief skit, he showed me how I would look "twenty years from now."

"You are eating, sleeping, sitting, and standing all wrong," he said. He gave me booklets to read and suggested visits to the physical therapist for exercises and a rigid diet plan.

I read the booklets, half-heartedly changed some of my habits, and sank further into depression until that fateful February when I suddenly realized if I didn't do something more, I would be feeling the breath of the Grim Reaper on my thickening neck.

I rolled out of bed, pulled on a pair of men's Adidas, purchased long ago at a discount store, struggled into sweatpants and shirt, and walked outside. In a few minutes, I found myself at my neighbor's door—she of the lithe body, the long blonde hair, and the marathon running ribbons. Though I didn't know her well, she had often accosted me with the words, "If you ever want to go running with me, just call." I had snickered to myself, wondering why this woman would want to waste time on a lumbering beginner like me.

But desperate needs call for desperate measures. I knocked at her door, and she appeared in her nightie. She must have recognized my desperation. She immediately changed into her running clothes, while informing me that she knew the perfect place. She led me to her car and drove me to the Yorktown High School track, a pleasingly private place, recessed and surrounded by trees.

I think we walked around once that day, my every joint creaking while she kept up a bright patter. For the next month she honked her horn for me every morning at nine. It was to take me several months to realize what a sacrifice it was on her part—runners simply don't suffer walkers gladly. My neighbor stayed with me until she was sure I was hooked enough to go on my own, and then she ran off.

During the first year I worked up to one hour a day, three miles an hour, four or five days a week. I was not on a diet, but exercise was changing my eating habits. I stopped snacking, started drinking more water. At the end of the first year, I had dropped thirty-two pounds.

My ruddy complexion and my energetic smile caused people to remark on my youth and vigor. My headaches didn't disappear entirely, but they lessened. The electrical currents and numbness in my fingers disappeared. Whereas previously I had needed to tote extra shoes everywhere, I now found my feet had strengthened enough to stand the same pair all day.

A surprising benefit of being a diligent walker was the fact that I stopped worrying about the weather. Since leaving Utah's hardy clime, I had taken on the habits of those who depend on air conditioning in the summer and furnaces in the winter, never venturing out in extreme weather. Now, if the car conked out in snow, I could walk. I didn't mind if flakes fell or water made walking a bit slippery, I was regaining the joy children take in seasonal changes. I could detect snow early enough to make it to the track before it fell. Then I would put on boots and make a little path. I felt somehow connected to my pioneer forebears.

During my first trail-blazing year, I met with some derision and disbelief. One fall day as I was rounding the third mile, I passed a man in a brown suit and hat who was munching an apple and watching me. Finally, he took the apple out of his mouth long enough to remark, "Is that all you ever do—walk?"

Surprised that my activity would attract any attention, let alone derision, I was not quick-witted enough to shoot back, "Is that all you ever do—watch?"

Runners at the track would run up to me, panting and gasping, as if my answer were important to their well-being, and ask, "Why don't you run?" It was simpler to be laconic. "Because I don't want to."

I could have told them that I believe walking is the best exercise for people who have heretofore been sedentary, who have health problems, or who think housework is a workout. It also has the advantage of being low key. You can sneak up on it before your psyche knows and tries to turn it into a program. I could have taken up swimming, or I could have joined the Mighty Mean Mothers Soccer Team in my neighborhood, but I am just not athletic. My doctor warned me against jogging because my flat feet and extra weight could lead to arthritic knees.

One day, quite by accident, I won second place in a speed-walking contest. The Potomac Seniors were at the track with various athletic contests for middle-aged folk. A friend saw me and talked me into entering. She gave me a brief demonstration of the skewed gait, and I was off. The result was a second place medal, the first medal of my entire life.

Proudly, I wore it to church and used it in my Relief Society lesson on fitness. I demonstrated my walk down the aisles of the chapel and challenged the women to take up whatever exercise they had left behind for whatever reason. During the next few months, I was gratified to hear from many that they were jogging, swimming, doing aerobics, and, yes, walking.

One of these women, a native of Arlington and a dance professor at Amherst College, invited me to walk with her on her summer and winter vacations. She would jog first, then walk with me to cool down. Another friend, an art historian in her seventies, started walking with me. We three sometimes walked together. Talk about a mobile education! Among the three of us, we knew enough about dance, art, and literature to open a small university!

Ruth rehearsed her lectures on Chinese art in preparation for a tour to China. Andrea rehearsed her lectures for a new course combining anatomy, physiology, and kinesiology. I opined on writing and editing. Andrea was inspired to write an essay on her reasons for becoming a dancer instead of a writer. Andrea and I signed up for some of Ruth's art tours. They both read my works in *Dialogue* and *Exponent II*.

This points up one of the advantages of walking—you can talk and walk at the same time. We three were different ages, at different physical stages, and we walked at different speeds, but we learned to adjust to one another.

From Andrea, the dancer, I learned that there are only a few exercises that benefit every muscle. This accounts for the fact that even though I lost thirty pounds during my first year of walking, my stomach was still flabby, and so were my upper arms. But walking is an especially good aerobic exercise, and it leads to a feeling of well-being and self-control.

It also did something more for me. During an eye exam, my ophthalmologist pronounced me a "glaucoma suspect" and told me to return in a few days for an in-depth exam. I went to the track to walk off my anxiety, praying and imagining the "worst that could happen." When I went back for the test, the doctor said I was back to normal. Since then, I have realized the benefit of the track for stress reduction.

The track represented even more than physical and mental health, it was an inspiration for art. Andrea's walking inspired her to create a dance called "To Be Danced While Jogging around the Yorktown Track." This became the centerpiece for her next concert at Amherst and received favorable reviews in the newspapers.

One day I described to Andrea the concept of the mandala, as I wanted to use it in a book of women's essays I was editing. A circle or a sphere, usually divided into four parts, the mandala is a healing, energy-giving symbol appearing in many different cultures. Jung discovered it in the dreams of his patients and defined it as a symbol of "the self, the wholeness of the personality." It is present today in art, religion, and psychology. As we discussed this during our walk, Andrea made an apt connection. Oval-shaped, circling the grassy baseball and soccer field, the track had become a healing mandala for us.

One morning in early June, Andrea and I walked in silence for a few minutes before noticing a lovely maple tree growing out of the center of the track. "It was not here yesterday!" we laughed.

Now it looked as if we were being repaid for our diligence. *A Tree Grows in Brooklyn* was now A Tree Grows in the Center of Our Mandala! What a wonderful symbol of rebirth. No matter that the tree was simply a farewell prank of the high school graduating class, it placed the seal of approval on everything the track had come to mean to us.

[1982]

# IV
# REACHING OUT

# ACROSS THE
# GENERATIONS

I had to pinch myself. I was actually standing in the rose garden at the Roosevelt home in Hyde Park, New York, staring at Roosevelt faces—sons, grandchildren, great-grandchildren of FDR and Eleanor, my childhood heroes. As the family and friends of the family stepped forward to place wreaths before the marble markers at the gravesite, I remembered listening to FDR's fireside chats on the radio, long ago in Utah. My father, then a blacksmith helper on the railroad, believed that FDR's patrician tones represented the voice of a savior. I became so enamored of the voice that, when the radio announced his death some years later, I went out into the orchard to cry and write in my diary. FDR seemed like a member of the family, and I connected his policies and programs with the war's end and my own rosy hopes for the future. Eleanor Roosevelt was the better half of the country, the woman who went where no one else dared to go. I did not think of her as strange or funny, the way some of my contemporaries did. She spoke for the oppressed in a quavery voice that I grew to believe was the voice of a saint.

"Everybody here is a Roosevelt but me," I told myself. I had been invited to this centennial celebration of Eleanor's birth as a guest of Esther Peterson, who was there as a speaker. It did seem that everyone here had either Eleanor's prominent mouth or FDR's brilliant smile. These were strong genetic markers that set the Roosevelts apart as aristocracy. But it was not so much an aristocracy of affluence as an aristocracy of service. Eleanor was the supreme symbol of this—the gawky, unloved orphan of the family, who had become, in the words of Harry Truman, "the first lady of the world."

The group in the rose garden moved on to Val-Kill, a few miles away, for the dedication of the Eleanor Roosevelt National Historic

Site. Val-Kill, Eleanor's home, had been saved from the wreckers by local citizens' groups and grandchildren who recognized that the simplicity and unpretentious pattern of her life were best represented by this group of simple stone and wood buildings. A cottage, a swimming pool, a barbecue pit, and sleeping rooms for guests provided quiet places to think, to plan, and to entertain. The Val-Kill program, along with the First Day stamp ceremony, was followed by a convocation at nearby Vassar College, where papers, workshops, speeches and dinners bore the theme, "The vision of Eleanor Roosevelt—past, present, and future." These often moving memorials sounded one note over and over again: Eleanor had never refused the call to public service. Admirers and students gathered at Val-Kill and Vassar were challenged to follow her.

Many years before, Esther Peterson had adopted Eleanor as mentor and model in her own dedication to service. Her experience in labor causes and women's rights led to paths already trodden by Eleanor. They first met at White House receptions and again at Val-Kill, but it was Esther's work as assistant secretary of labor under President Kennedy that brought them together. Eleanor was chairman and Esther vice-chairman of the President's Commission on the Status of Women (1961–63). Eleanor had responded to the call with the words, "This will be the last big thing I do." Indeed, she died just before the report was published.

Esther's memories of the planning discussions at Val-Kill formed part of her tribute at the banquet. "Whenever I speak on issues that mean so much to me, I feel Mrs. Roosevelt standing at my side." They had prepared the status report during meetings at Val-Kill where representatives of the bipartisan commission discussed the rights, the sufferings, and the potential of America's women.

The report and the work of the commission are little-appreciated today. Although Arthur Schlesinger gave the report just due in his opening address at Vassar, papers presented later downplayed Eleanor's contributions because she had not been an early supporter of the ERA. Calling her a "reformer" rather than a "feminist," the papers showed little understanding of her international stature as a champion of women. "The will of a woman is the strongest force in the world," she once said.

Do today's women understand that the work of Eleanor and Esther paved the way for them?

Esther is almost a generation younger than Eleanor, and I am almost a generation younger than Esther. I ask myself, "Does my generation have the strength that Esther's and Eleanor's had? And will my generation teach our children to appreciate the doors they opened for *us*?"

Eleanor Roosevelt's contribution to women and to the entire cause of human rights is vast. How could one woman have defended these rights so tirelessly for so long? Part of her motivation was her religious faith, a fact I had only dimly perceived before hearing the testimonies of those who knew her personally. One of these was Pauli Murray, a New Deal civil rights lawyer and black activist, who, after finishing that distinguished career, donned the robes of an Episcopal priest. She paid tribute to Eleanor's deep faith in Christ that had converted her to her own late-life mission. She and others emphasized the importance of keeping Eleanor's image bright, not with tributes, which would have embarrassed her, but with actions.

As I listened, I asked myself what the message could be for Mormon women. Certainly, we can continue to excavate the contributions of our pioneer mothers and we can celebrate contemporary foremothers like Algie Eggertsen Ballif, Esther's sister. In her own way, Algie was a symbol worthy of Eleanor. When I walked into the Eleanor wing of the Roosevelt Library at Hyde Park, my first thought was of Algie. A crystal sculpture dedicated to Eleanor is inscribed, "Instead of cursing the dark, she chose to light a candle." Algie's sight was almost gone when she died. When a stroke dimmed her lively mind, she laughed at the demons of darkness. That laughter, combined with unfailing energy for the causes of Mormon women, kept her active for eighty-eight years and posted her at the center of a group of women who bear some of the most distinguished names in Mormondom. Educated, talented, many of them in their seventies and eighties, they call themselves the Alice Reynolds Women's Forum. They meet to speak, to listen, and to engage in debate, usually in a room they funded themselves on the BYU campus.

In 1980, I met with the Alice Reynolds Forum in my role as editor of *Dialogue*. Nineteen women, two husbands, and two of my children gathered in a circle around Helen Candland Stark. Helen began by showing the group an egg timer, admonishing them to be brief, and stating the purpose, "to help Mary Bradford in her awesome task of speaking for the sisterhood of the church in the forthcoming women's issue of *Dialogue*." She asked that we all "speak our small truths." The women talked both of their frustrations with the church and their strong commitment to it. They described disappointed attempts to meet with church leaders and their sorrow at the excommunication of Sonia Johnson. They spoke of campaigns for public office and local reform movements they had sponsored. Single women, widowed and divorced women spoke of both acceptance and loneliness. Married women paid tribute to their husbands. All expressed love for the young women of the church and the generation they hoped would be spared the need to fight old battles all over again.

Algie Ballif was the glowing fireside of the evening. She and another sister, Thelma Weight, described discussions in her parents' home where "we children were never hushed up. We heard things, and we listened, and we asked questions. This has never left us." Algie thanked the group for their honesty, for their willingness to share their deepest feelings. She celebrated them for their diversity and went on to praise the "diversity in the human heart." "We are having struggles," Algie said, "and we don't want to give up those struggles. They are very valuable." At that moment I understood a little better the source of energy in the room. Algie, Thelma, Helen, and the others were survivors who were actually glad for the strength and opportunity that struggle brings. I felt inadequate in their presence. I asked myself, "Do they also serve who only sit and write?"

But Algie's praise of diversity gave me courage. If I, and others far more eloquent than I, persist in the difficult art of speaking and writing the truth, we may yet light a candle for our daughters—and our sons.

[1984]

# THIS PRECIOUS STONE

*This precious stone / set in the silver sea, This blessed plot, this earth / this realm / this England.—Shakespeare, Richard II*

As a child I lived in books and scenes from books, beginning with nursery rhymes with their rolling green hills and funny-faced pigs, to the Arthurian legends and Robert Louis Stevenson, then on to Hardy, Dickens, Austen, and the Brontës. I was introduced to Shakespeare early and was never intimidated by him even when he mystified me. Therefore, when I actually stood in the English countryside and London's city streets, they were blindingly familiar. I seemed to be looking at the scenery through colors not quite of this world. I suppose there are yellow wildflowers deep down in the grasses of Runnymede and under the boughs of Pooh's Hundred Acre Wood and the meadows of Devon to make the green of England so bright. That and the rain that falls gently almost every morning and clears up every evening.

Touring Oxford at dusk, with its golden towers against the sky, organ music sounding through the walls, the spreading trees inside the enclosed courtyard, I surprised myself by crying out, "Oh! I've wasted my life!" How could I explain the conviction that I, a middle-aged English major and Anglophile visiting Oxford for the first time, had been born in the wrong country at the wrong time?

Regret, however, hadn't kept me from joining my daughter Lorraine during the last three weeks of her BYU semester abroad. I stayed with the directors—my friends, the Marshalls, the Englands, and the Paxmans—in one of the tall, golden rowhouses near Hyde Park in London that comprise the BYU Center. The other one housed the students and their classrooms.

After settling in with Gene and Charlotte England, I joined the student bus tour to southern England. Stonehenge, our first stop, didn't look nearly as prehistoric as I had imagined. Instead of dark, foreboding pillars, lit from behind by the timid sun, as pictured on postcards and in Thomas Hardy, there was a visitors center and a fence rising incongruously between me and the storied altars. It had been raised against souvenir hunters who have been carrying off the monument, a stone at a time. We found an angle from which to take a picture and tried to imagine a lone and dreary plain with nobody but Druids to disturb the calm.

I had expected, like John Fowles in his *Enigma of Stonehenge,* to be able to run across "the cropped greensward" to "climb, scramble, squeeze through stone pillars." But he says that people have not been allowed to walk up to the monument since well before his birth. I was taken with the stone itself, so hard, so blue. I thought of the Arthurian legends that claim the monoliths were brought from Ireland through the magic of Merlin. I thought of the legend of "The Sword in the Stone"—the sword being the masculine, warlike side of life, and the stone, the feminine and peaceful earth.

In a suitably dreary drizzle at Lyme Regis, Gene England read to us from another Fowles masterpiece, *The French Lieutenant's Woman.* In Hardy's Shaftesbury, we climbed Cobbled Gold Hill, high above Blackmoor heath. At Salisbury Cathedral, we gave obeisance to one of the world's tallest spires, then on to Exeter, where the students put up at a hostel and Lorraine and I at a bed and breakfast.

The bed was cold and clammy but the breakfast was hot and tasty. Over bacon, ham, sausage, eggs, tomatoes, cereal, and juice, we talked to our hostess about the bombings she survived during World War II. I thought of Virginia Woolf mourning the bombing of her London house, her frail sanity finally broken. Rubbing a stone as a talisman, she walked into the river Ouse.

Next morning's drive to the coast was a dream of English villages. Our bus stopped at Clovelley, which is built into a rock. The main street is so steep that the only vehicle that can make the grade is a hand-drawn, wooden delivery sled. We walked down past Della Robbia doorways and a little Methodist church that had just finished a "Festival of Flowers" to honor the royal marriage of Charles and Diana. The village was all alcoves and shops tumbling into each other, clean and pretty and ending at the water's edge. We bought some Devon "clotted cream" to take with us. It is very thick, beaten one step beyond whipped cream, one step short of butter, and good on everything.

The directors of this trip seemed to believe in the hit-run method of sightseeing. The glorious Wells Cathedral was worth twenty minutes. The Valley of the Rocks, with its twin villages of Lynmouth and Lynton, rated half an hour. Heading for the Cornwall Coast, Monroe Paxman discoursed on King Arthur's Glastonbury appearing in the distance, and Shirley Paxman announced that the rabbits we could see in the undulating fields were the stars of *Watership Down*. Gene read to us from Coleridge at the town of Porlock. Stopping on Pickwick Street at Southwark gave us an excuse to look for Dickensian characters in a nearby pub.

I didn't really mind the speed, I felt so lucky to be there. During all of it, I felt my vocabulary improved, my brain cells rejuvenated, my speech centers oiled. I found myself making puns and remembering names. I grew patriotic about my language. As the cliché goes, in England even little children speak perfect English. Emma, the four-year-old daughter of the center's resident managers, when asked how she is feeling, replies, "Not well, thank you. I have a nasty cold." Oh! the tone of her British voice that shows an appreciation of language she is not aware of yet, the richness of accent, the lilt of varied word choices.

Back in London, Lorraine and I took our own private tour down Fleet Street past the Lincoln Inns and "The Cheshire Cheese," where Dr. Johnson and Dickens used to eat. We reached the remodeled Covent Garden, where we ate quiche at an outdoor cafe and watched a flame swallower and juggler. From there, we visited the National Portrait Gallery and more old friends from English literature.

Old friends all:

> Smiling, frowning, leaping from the wall. I knew them
> pressed into pages,
> connected through the ages,
> now joined in colors and cadenced
> tapestries of space,
> dynasties of Tudors, tutors, a race
> of kings and commoners, admirals, trumpets
> sounding through words half-remembered, strumpets

like Lady Hamilton, bidding me to Nelson's side,
bidding me abide.
I do. Then I stride,
then sit and stare.
I look for lines of care
in Dickens' beauty, in George Eliot's jaw,
I find some faces raw,
like Epstein's ravaged carving,
like Virginia Woolf's starving.
I am finally sated abated.
                    —From my diary, June 10, 1983

We took a bus to the Tate, but when we got off and started walking, it was three miles before we found it. My feet were burning, but William Blake was worth it. To walk into his exhibit is to enter a hushed, cool shrine. My first time to see Blake's art, I was immediately plunged into his visionary world. Elohim, with a puzzled, angry expression, appears to be creating Adam through the coils of the snake.

Lorraine's favorites are the pre-Raphaelites and Whistler. I said, "Let's sit here and stare at the Whistlers or perhaps whistle at the Starers." We giggled and went for ice cream, foregoing the apples we brought with us.

This time we were able to catch a subway and a bus that took us to Royal Albert Hall to hear the Sunday Evening Orchestral Concert. The New Symphony Orchestra played romantic, old standards we had played for Lorraine on our first phonograph years ago—"Scheherazade," "Finlandia," "William Tell." It seemed only yesterday that she was impatiently turning them off. Now, she sat enraptured on our top balcony perch just like Blake's painting, *Spirit Vaulting from a Cloud.*

Next morning, Gene woke me to ask if I would "take care of Bernard Brown." Bernard Brown is a British Shakespearean actor and a convert to the church of six years. I knew of him through an article submitted to *Dialogue* a few years before.

While the students and faculty prepared for finals, I talked with Bernard until time for his presentation to the students in the evening. He is a charming man in the diffident, courteous British way, gray eyes, light hair, about forty years old.

We talked for some time about conditions in England—especially the high unemployment. When his company, the venerable Old Vic, closed down, he moved to South Africa where there is much demand for Shakespeare. Now he was back in England where he was getting some Shakespearean parts on television, but hardly enough to support himself and his family. Since joining the church, he was no longer attracted by parts in certain modern plays. He said the demand for his art was dwindling in England.

I was puzzled by this. Hadn't I been attending the theater every night, sometimes twice in one day, at ridiculously low prices? Hadn't I loved every minute of it?

He explained that for every actor in a hit play, there are ten or twenty unemployed actors. His ambition was to emigrate to America—specifically to Provo and BYU. He had visited there and been greeted with enthusiasm by students and faculty.

"You mean the grass is greener elsewhere? How could the grass be greener than in England!" I said. I described my little epiphany at Oxford with the overwhelming conviction that I had wasted my life by studying in out-of-the-way Utah. He asserted that America is vast and there is room for all. He had applied to teach at BYU and was still hoping to be hired there.

As he talked, I remembered other images of life in England, works by "angry young men" like Braine and Osborne, novels and plays that painted the grubby, class-ridden society that kept people in their place, especially if the place was poverty.

Bernard had lived part of my dream, but that hadn't guaranteed happiness. The "tight little island" seemed to be shrinking as his conversion to Mormonism expanded his vision. My term at BYU as instructor of English and my education at the University of Utah sounded appealing to Bernard. I tried to express my envy, my Anglophilia, my longings for the world of books and the landscapes of my imagination.

But I could see that they couldn't compare to his dream of The Promised Land.

That night, as he performed his one-man Shakespearean medley for the students, and I saw him open like a flower to their spellbound attention, I devoutly hoped for the fruition of his wish—to act in America, to teach at BYU.

A week later, while all the students except Lorraine were on tour in Scotland, another actor arrived at the center: James Arrington from Utah with his one-man show, "Brother Brigham." Lorraine and I had our orders: "Take care of James."

This was good duty. We are long-time friends and fans of James and his work. After greeting him at Gatwick, riding with him on the train, and helping to carry his luggage on the subway, we showed him his bed. The next day, we went with him to Hyde Park chapel. The chairs had been set up for the performance the next night, but the stage was full of debris. It was obvious that the stage lights had not been used in this century, and furniture for the set was nowhere to be found. In spite of Gene's weekly announcements at church, the authorities had not understood that the production was an actual stage play and not a mere "reading." So Lorraine and I went back to the center and talked to Leonard, the resident manager and member of the bishopric, who happened to be a carpenter and all-round handyman. He built a bench and a sign for the stage set and fixed the lights. Then we went in search of an instant print company.

During these preparations, I chatted with the woman in charge of public communications for the church in London. She would not be coming to the performance, she informed me, because she lived forty minutes away by tube. This baffled me. I told her that in Washington, we think nothing of traveling forty minutes or more for a good performance. She was unmoved, and I thought it ludicrous that I should be standing there telling the public communications expert what was going on in her own ward. My vision of life among the Mormons of England was being revised. I had always imagined them ever at the ready, always up for the theater! Subsidized by the government, it is affordable, and I was able to go with Lorraine on student rush tickets to almost everything: *Cats, Nicholas Nickleby* (all eight hours), *Evita, Educating Rita,* as well as a marvelous production of *Swan Lake* by the Stuttgart Ballet.

I was also frustrated in my attempts to reach the few British *Dialogue* subscribers. When I finally connected on the phone with two of them, they told me distances were too great for them to meet me or to attend "Brother Brigham."

When James informed us that he had chosen Lorraine as ticket-taker and me as backstage light and sound manager, I panicked. Long ago, when drama was part of my college major, I had worked as a stagehand, but never had I been entrusted with such a responsible position as keeper of the lights!

"James, not only am I the world's original klutz, but my hands aren't big enough to reach across the light panel." He promised to simplify everything so that even a klutz could do it. The next night as he applied his beard, he clued me about my cues at the light panel. I felt clammy. What if I should black him out during his most dramatic moment?

As I marked the script and tried to figure out how to push all three "generals" at once, Lorraine signaled to me that the students had returned from Scotland and were looking for seats in a packed house. I saw my chance. I ran down and grabbed Jody England, a former drama major. "You're in luck!" I said. I dragged her backstage, pointed to the light panel, and said, "You've been chosen to run the lights."

She was delighted. And James, though suffering from jet lag and hunger, and nervous from the hectic preparations, went on, while Jody and I crouched near the lights and came within a breath of blacking out the scene where Brigham accepts the Mantle of the Prophet.

James won the audience, as he usually does, and the leadership begged him to stay and perform again. But he was off to Leicester for the weekend, where the stake president and his wife were hosting the performance, a fireside, and a sacrament meeting. President and Sister Jones knew how to deliver a crowd. James was a success.

The next morning we went to nearby Nottingham to see Sherwood Forest. I wasn't expecting much. Guide books had lamented the loss of the expansive forest of olden times. Now only a few trees commemorate Robin Hood and the royal huntsmen who had once roamed there. So I was not prepared for my feelings when I looked at the giant oaks, some hollow enough to hold a man, as Gene soon proved. Gene and James argued briefly about whether the outdoors is better than the indoors, with James claiming that to be outdoors is better than to read about it. Gene pointed out that if we hadn't read about Robin Hood and Sherwood Forest, we wouldn't know what we were seeing. I pronounced them both right. The trees would be impressive even if they had not been worshipped by the Druids, but somehow it helped to know, via Robert Graves in *The White Goddess,* that "the Oak was the tree of Zeus, Jupiter, Hercules, Thor, and all the other Thundergods, and Jehovah . . . the tree of endurance and triumph." The Major Oak was about half a mile away, and it was getting late. We raced each other up the path. The magnificent tree was worth the trip. Thirty-three feet in circumference, it is almost five hundred years old. Even if you didn't feel like worshipping it, you could find shelter in its thick limbs and the soft ground beneath.

At the center that night, James, with his usual stamina, performed once more for the students—this time from his original, two-person play, "Farley's Family Reunion." This hit was followed by student tributes to their leaders, with a response in the form of a Greek dance by Monroe Paxman.

So, the semester ended and I was left to ponder its effects during my flight home. It would be silly to spend even a minute more in regret. I am still young enough to appreciate beauty where I find it. And England in all its fading glory is still a magical peepstone for me.

[1981]

# MY TEN-DAY MISSION

Out of the banana groves and rice fields, out of the mud huts, bamboo "nipa huts," and tin squatter houses grow the vivid flowers known as the Philippine people. Given to much laughter, tears, and music, they welcomed me with the words, "You are very beautiful, Sister. Like mother like daughter!" Invariably they laughed and added good-natured comments about my figure. Lorraine had warned me of this, assuring me that such remarks as "You are fat, Sister!" and "You are so beeg!" are not derogatory. On the contrary, to be overweight in the United States is to be fortunate and attractive in the Philippines. The Saints in the Philippines often go without food, but they are hungry not only for food but for knowledge. As one young man put it, "When I am hungry, I read the scriptures, and then I am full."

They were grateful that we chose to visit them in their homes. "We thought you would want to go to the resorts instead," they said, at the same time apologizing for their poverty. "We are poor, Sister, but we are trying to improve."

## Cebu City

Lorraine met me at the airport with two elders from the mission home. After a confusing three hours in Manila where I had overtipped a few people, I was relieved to see her, vibrant in lavender dress and missionary name tag. (I have been known to deprecate the name tag on the grounds that it "makes sitting ducks of the missionaries," but this trip taught me to think of it as a talisman that could guide us through customs and other confusions.)

The elders drove us to the mission home, a beautiful mansion in the wealthy suburb of Beverly Hills. Next door to a Chinese temple, it nestles in the luxuriant trees and bushes of the tropics—bougainvillea, poincianna, crepe myrtle, and of course, coconut and banana groves.

The view across the hills revealed another more elaborate Chinese temple, bright red among the pink and yellow flowers.

I was welcomed by President Boulter and his wife and introduced to other missionaries. As the sweat rolled off my face, they assured me that I was now enjoying the relatively cool monsoon season. I had read about the heavy rains and typhoons and was not comforted.

The next morning, Lorraine announced that she was calling me on a "ten-day mission." I was to become her companion in all five of the areas where she had labored—Cebu, Bacolad, Valencia, Tanjay, and Iloilo. When I asked how my trip could be compared to a mission, she replied, "You will go everywhere missionaries go, only in a shorter time. People think missionary work is all proselyting. They don't realize how much of it is visiting members, shoring them up, and meeting their neighbors."

Lorraine reported that President Boulter, in her final interview, had asked her to name the best thing about her mission. "I said that I had learned to recognize God in all that I did. He has led me by the hand." She also said she needed me to share her mission. Our trip would build a bridge from mission life to home. Later she showed me a diary entry: "I desperately need to share with Mom all the beautiful experiences of my mission—to review and analyze and, mostly, to allow her to experience what I went through. I want my mother—my closest friend—to understand."

We began in the slums of Cebu City, well below the exclusive world of Beverly Hills. After a brief, hair-raising trip in a jeepney, we found ourselves in the center of the oldest city in the Philippines. Discovered by Magellan in the 1400s, it had been dedicated to the glory of Spain and King Philip. It was a hybrid of ancient, rundown buildings and streets filled with T-shirted young people and blaring radios. Western pop songs led the hit parade with "We Are the World" as number one. We stopped to look at a group of comic book addicts, who for a mere two pesos were allowed to rent a comic book and sit in a kind of sidewalk classroom, cordoned from the traffic, to read during the lunch hour.

We had arranged to meet with Sister Esplin—Lorraine's Cebu companion—and Sister Matthews, who were also being released. They went with us to the apartment where they had lived. It was shabby and hot, but luxurious compared to homes of the members. Lorraine broke it to me that the missionaries had lived with rats until one chewed the coat off a teddy bear and the elders were conscripted as a rodent swat team.

We hopped onto a jeepney for the trip to Figueroa Street, home of Lorraine's converts. They had followed the lead of one Sister Abajo, who, after her own conversion, opened her home for ongoing missionary work with her neighbors. I was looking forward to meeting the writers of some charming thank-you letters we had received after sending hymn books to the "Figueroa Street Choir."

I thought I knew how Figueroa Street would look—like festive Olivera Street in downtown L.A., quaint, Spanish, and colorful. In fact, Lorraine's enthusiastic letters had made her Cebu City period sound like one big lark. Even being caught on the street during a typhoon sounded like fun. I was unprepared for the sights, sounds, and especially the smells of the real thing: fumes from burning rubber combined with the smoke of food being cooked on open braziers, and a stench that I couldn't place until we jumped over a wide gray ditch to climb the steps to Sister Abajo's house. This was a "gunge ditch," slang for open sewage.

I would soon discover that almost everything in the Philippines is open. The houses of the poor are built of bamboo, leftover wood and metal, even cardboard. The transportation system depends on jeeps and buses open on all sides. The popular "tricycles" are nothing more than motorcycles with decorated sidecars. And, looking downright medieval, are the open buggies drawn by gaunt horses. Open too are the hearts of the people, who live so close together that almost nothing can be locked away or kept secret.

Because Sister Abajo's house is on stilts, it provides shelter for another family in the dirt below. I could see babies with sores on their bodies playing there. Sister Abajo, or "Sister Bradford's Philippine mother," who is about my age, greeted us with tears and kisses. She is rearing two children from her second marriage with help from an eighteen-year-old daughter from her first marriage. Her hut, which she rebuilt with her own hands after the last typhoon, was colorfully painted and decorated in honor of the departing missionaries. Her hand-crocheted jeepney decorations were strung about the turquoise and pink walls. She had covered the ceiling with flowered gift wrap. A built-in corner shelf was candlelit like a shrine, with a picture of President Kimball where Saint Nemo, patron saint of Catholic Cebu, had been. A curtain separated the living room from the bedroom, and a wooden deck connected her house to that of the neighbors.

Her small daughters—aged seven and five—attend elementary school, she told me proudly. Their tuition comes out of her meager earnings from sales of the jeepney decorations. After complimenting them on their written schoolwork, I swallowed both a bottled orange drink and a Sprite. Lorraine introduced me to the people who were quietly filtering into the room—young men in their early twenties, a few young women, and some slightly older couples like the bishop and his wife, and the Relief Society president and her family.

I was the oldest one there. In fact, the bishop's wife was surprised to learn my advanced age. All the women seemed to think me both younger and prettier than they, and they were curious about my economic situation. Did I work? At what? When I tried to describe my writing and editing contracts, they were puzzled. Was I paid well for such services? I didn't tell them how unhappy I had been with my meager recompense over the years. I merely admitted that I had been well paid for this (entirely expendable) work.

They described the Catch-22 that keeps their people out of work. What used to be a public school system has virtually disappeared so that only those who can pay attend. Without jobs, of course, there is no money for school. Without schooling, few can qualify for jobs. One young convert had been disowned by his Catholic parents and could no longer afford schooling. Some have opened small jewelry and refreshment stands. The family of the Relief Society president owes its refrigerator and stove to their daughter's American marriage. Some men lose their jobs after they join the church, because they can no longer drink and carouse with fellow workers. Some women bring in money through handwork and domestic service. Many young people plan to serve missions supported by the church.

After the room had filled to overflowing, and we had eaten the delicacies that had suddenly appeared—fried bananas, vegetable candy, sticky rice, and a kind of sweet enchilada called *lumpia*—Lorraine said she would tape their songs and testimonies. So for the next two hours, we were serenaded a cappella by solos, trios, and quartets, singing American pop songs and romantic ballads like "I Left My Heart in San Francisco." Most of them had very agreeable voices, some were musical comedy material. The whole program wound up with hymn singing and the Figueroa Street theme song, "Love at Home."

Next, in a combination of English and Cebuano, Lorraine introduced the testimonies. As a doting parent, I couldn't help but notice her empathy for suffering and willingness to reach out. I remembered an incident from her fourth grade year, when black children were being integrated into our district by being bused from the other end of the county. I learned from her teacher that a long scratch on Lorraine's arm was the result of an attack by one of the new students and that Lorraine had begged for clemency for the little girl. "She didn't mean it. She just needs love."

It was difficult to say goodbye to the folks of Figueroa Street. As I mingled my tears with theirs, they wiped mine away with their hands. Walking out with us, they found a taxi, and hovered over it as we slowly pulled away. I shall always remember their faces pressed to the windows as they promised to meet us again—"Maybe in the celestial kingdom."

At five o'clock the next morning, we took a plane to Dumaguete on the island of Negros and a hotel with the unlikely name, The North Pole. Located on the beach across from a muddy squatters' settlement, it had a seedy grandeur like something out of Somerset Maugham. Ragged red carpet covered the beautiful mahogany staircase, and a kidney-shaped swimming pool could be discerned among the banana and dieffenbachia trees in back. We ate breakfast in the deserted dining room and prepared for our visit to Valencia and Tanjay by reading written testimonies the members had inscribed in Lorraine's journal. Then we hailed a tricycle and rode to town.

We walked through the open-air market on the way to the post office where we mailed a succinct postcard to Chick. This trip had been his Christmas present to me, along with a ten-page book filled with step-by-step information about schedules, tickets, hotels, and exchange rates. Lorraine had burst out laughing when she saw her father's "thesis," but she joined me in poring over it every night at bedtime.

## Valencia

Lorraine's most primitive area, Valencia, had a beauty not unlike the movies I remembered from my youth, *South of Pango Pango* with Jon Hall or *On the Road to Singapore* with Dorothy Lamour. Its green freshness was a relief after stifling Cebu. Pigs, goats, carabaos, and chickens peered at us as we putted up the hill. Missionary work moved so slowly in Valencia that the church had almost decided to close it. But the day Lorraine was transferred, all four of the families she had been teaching were baptized. She hoped to find them still active.

After tramping through the fields for a couple of hours, we found only one member at home. But what a member! Seraphina Kho, aged sixty going on twenty, one of the few Filipinas I met who actually owned her own property with its fruit, flowers, and coconut trees. Hers was one of the few houses I saw that was not open to the elements. The high wooden door could be securely locked. A recent convert, she had studied several evangelical religions before settling on Mormonism.

While Sister Kho saved me from drowning in my own sweat by serving Sprite and orange soda, she had a visit from a neighbor—a swarthy, talkative man loudly lamenting the loss of his *copra* (dried coconut) crop. It had just burned up, along with two dryers used to prepare the coconut for export. Looking worried, Sister Kho promised the loan of her dryers. He declared that he did not suspect arson but would report it to the authorities anyway. He went on to regale us with the story of his life, beginning with his miraculous recovery from a crib fire that left his face permanently scarred. Later, he had spent two years in Saudi Arabia earning money to send to his wife, while at the same time keeping his throat from being slit by his nefarious employers. But instead of saving his money and awaiting his return, his wife had spent it on riotous living. He is philosophical about his divorce and continues to trust God.

Sister Kho scolded him mildly for his smoking and seemed relieved when he offered us a ride in his jeep. He dropped us near the missionary apartment that doubles as a church. As we started down the road again, we were hailed by a jolly woman carrying a basket of tiny green fruit. Sister Vendiola was out selling *calamanci*, citrus that looks and tastes like miniature limes. She walked with us to our next stop—the

Catholic orphanage, or Friendship House—the scene of many of Lorraine's "Christian service hours." She had taught dance and aerobics to the children and played with the babies.

The building is a thatched A-frame in green hills across from a matching church. We were greeted by a nun in a nut-brown habit the exact color of her skin and eyes. She was not the nun Lorraine had written me about, the one who was transferred because she had asked for the missionary lessons. The nun reported on the children that had recently been adopted and the ones who hadn't. When Lorraine asked to see the babies, she led us to a room with four cribs. One was asleep on his stomach, his little bruised bottom covered with ointment. The nun told us that they were victims of child abuse. Lorraine and I took turns rocking and holding the other three. Of course, they stopped fretting and stared up at us with numb longing. It was difficult to put them down, but it was time to catch the jeepney for the trip down the mountain. Sister Vendiola gave us calamanci to suck on and begged us to come back later to see the members we had missed. I didn't see how we could, having planned for only one day in Valencia and one in Tanjay, but Lorraine promised anyway.

We ate dinner at a restaurant on the beach next to our hotel. That is, Lorraine ate dinner. I was still afflicted with a mighty thirst that for, some reason, caused me to order a banana split.

The next morning we were awakened by Sister Kho, who had traveled from Valencia to bring us fruit—rhomotons, which look like bright red cockle-burrs. Underneath the skins are slippery white segments that are sweet as long as you don't bite down on the large almond-shaped seed in the middle! Refusing to stay for breakfast and holding her purse tightly under her arm, Sister Kho departed just a few minutes before the arrival of Sister Vendiola, who had come to deliver more calamanci and to inform us that the whole branch would be meeting at the missionary apartment in Valencia for delicacies even now being prepared. She, too, refused to sit down, departing as suddenly as she had come.

## Tanjay

The trip to Tanjay was negotiated on a rickety bus that also served as a delivery service. Not only were more people climbing on than it could safely hold, but it was stopping at numerous hamlets along the way to pick up quantities of rice flour and fruits to store on the roof. It was a slow circuitous trip, but a beautiful one. It followed the waterfront all the way, and we could see the water as well as thick green fields of rice. Such fields had puzzled me when I had seen them from the air. Lorraine explained that they were salt evaporation beds doubling as fish ponds.

We reached Tanjay at high noon and began a walk through town. Fortunately, we were armed with the most important items in our first-aid kits—umbrellas and handkerchiefs. When it wasn't raining, the sun boiled down so mercilessly that we always needed protection.

Turning in at the doorway of a commodious house unlike anything I had seen at our other stops, we greeted Erkie and Joann and their small child. They lived with her mother, who owns the home and supports them on her government clerical job. Erkie told us, however, that he was planning to leave wife and family for a two-year job in Kuwait.

As on Figueroa Street, neighborhood Mormons gathered to greet us and to pose for our camera. Lorraine recorded their songs and testimonies too, and we ate their sandwiches. Erkie, an active ward mission leader, expressed a thought that seemed plucked from my own mind: "We are going for quality, not quantity here. We don't worry about numbers and percentages. Too many join and then fall away. We are slowing down and looking for members who will stay with us."

We then walked through the town center with its striking Spanish cathedral dedicated to Santiago (Saint James), whose colorfully painted likeness appeared to be riding a bucking bronco atop the tiled roof. We stopped for another treat—boiled ice water at the missionary apartment—and joined forces with a lovely young Mormon woman who went with us to our other destinations in Tanjay. One of these was the branch office where Elder and Sister Neilsen were working. They too had lived with Lorraine and her companion. Jolly and energetic, Elder Neilsen announced, "I am seventy years old, and I feel like a dang kid!" They talked proudly of the coming dedication of the new chapel for which Lorraine had helped break ground, and walked with us to where it stood near the city center. All the members had worked on it, and it seemed to me its beauty exceeded the Mormon standard plan for chapels in the United States.

We visited another family in a nipa hut through the densest banana grove yet. This family was less poverty-stricken because the father had a job as a bank guard in the city. It seemed to me, though, that the needs of the people were overwhelming. I wondered how the church could keep up.

As we waited for the bus back to Dumaguete, I was assaulted by a colorful cacophony around me. A blood-curdling squeal went up at such a pitch it made my ears ring. *"FOR HEAVEN'S SAKE, WHAT IS IT?"*

"Hogs," Lorraine said. Yes, two large black hogs were being dragged down off the roof of a bus.

*"WHAT ARE THEY DOING TO THE POOR HOGS?"*

"They are getting ready to sell them," she said. "Most families try to raise at least one hog to sell."

All cities are noisy, but it seemed to me that the Philippine cities are too noisy for such gentle inhabitants. In the middle of Cebu or Manila, drivers make it clear that the horn is a car's most important feature. The people have a couple of signals besides honking horns—a certain clicking of the teeth and a soft hiss that, although light, carry remarkably well. They use these when climbing on or off a vehicle and also to attract the attention of the opposite sex. I was fascinated with these sounds because they could penetrate the din of the noisiest street. The people have also perfected the stare. In a jeepney, all fifteen or twenty riders would stare at us. At first, I was apprehensive, but I soon learned to smile in response. This would bring immediate answering smiles. They never tried to strike up a conversation.

It was dark by the time we reached Dumaguete again, and tricycles rarely go up the mountain after dark. Lorraine refused to listen to my pronouncement that we'd had enough for one day and should forego Valencia. She said the people would be waiting for us and that the Lord would find us a tricycle driver. This time she didn't stop to bargain for a lower fare.

It was raining lightly. As is the custom, our driver stopped at a gas station to buy gas enough for our trip and not one drop more. It carried us to a spot a few feet away from our destination. The driver agreed to wait until we made it to the door. Then he turned around and coasted down the hill.

We were not a moment too soon! After waiting two and a half hours, Lorraine's friends had given up and were starting for their homes. It was so dark I could barely see their flashing smiles. Practically the whole branch was there, including Lorraine's former housekeeper, a young woman with an alarming history. Seems that the minute she earns a few pesos to feed herself and her children, her good-for-nothing husband returns. He stays just long enough to make her pregnant and pocket her money.

We were served various rice and vegetable cakes and *boco*, which I mistook for milk with noodles floating in it. It was young coconut, Lorraine's favorite dish. After the food came the photographs, the taping, and the singing. Their reports were all encouraging except for the news that two mothers had left their families to do domestic work in Singapore. Brother Banlat, one of the husbands, had moved his family in with his sister and had become a tricycle driver. He offered us a ride back to our hotel, so we piled in with two of the women, while two children clung to Brother Banlat and two husbands followed on another motorcycle. Although we had used up their gas and probably most of their food for the week, they refused to let us pay. Later, Lorraine let me read her diary entry: "Mom said it used to seem like all the people looked just alike, but she knows now that each is distinct and different. All unique and beautiful in their own way."

We had to fly back to Cebu for a connecting flight to Bacolad, which is on the same island as Dumaguete but is more accessible by air. Bacolad was her first assignment.

## Bacolad

We arrived after dark. Porters and cab drivers here were more aggressive and didn't seem to understand that we did not need four people to carry our four bags. It was frightening to find ourselves in a small, sleazy hotel room with the porters all waiting for tips. When we explained that we couldn't tip them all, they merely laughed and left.

I awoke feeling uneasy. This was another area Lorraine had given me to believe was just short of paradise. And now the truth was out. There were even more rats and trash here than in Cebu. During her time, the elders had been tied up and robbed and mission leaders had stationed a guard at the sisters' apartment. As we picked our way through the mud, I clutched my purse in one hand and Lorraine with the other and comforted myself with the thought that if missionaries seek out only the best neighborhoods, they will never find the truly poor in spirit. Bacolad was the only stop on our itinerary that word of our coming had not somehow preceded us, so we made a surprise entrance at the Mormon compound. Beautiful faces looked out of rotting cardboard huts clustered around what appeared to be a used car lot. Lorraine said that they couldn't even afford bamboo for nipa huts. Though some of the men work repairing vehicles, most families have almost no income. Yet, the ugliness seemed to fall away in the hospitality of the moment. We found ourselves in the home of the Santillans, another bishop's family, with members dropping in. We were served two different kinds of bananas, large orange ones and small "finger" bananas, along with Lorraine's favorite fruit, guava. This bishop was an artist who taught drafting in a nearby school. The tiny room was hung with his Philippine landscapes. The Santillans introduced their children: Katharine, Joseph Smith, Hyrum Smith, and Oliver Cowdery. Joseph and Hyrum, aged five and three, sang a fifteen-minute medley of church songs. From there we dropped in on seventy-year-old Brother Tan. Partially paralyzed and cared for by his wife, he hadn't left his hut since he was baptized.

"Can't the members take him to church?" I asked.

"He would have to be carried all the way. They have no transportation and no money for cabs." But what about church welfare? As I looked around, my heart sank. Conditions were so depressed that church welfare was needed for more than transportation to meetings.

We, however, could afford a cab to the neighborhood of a newly renovated chapel in another of Lorraine's districts. Even though it glowed like a jewel in the rain, it depressed me, too. Shouldn't the money and labor for that building have been used to feed and house the members instead? The bishop was inside helping to ready the building for the visit of three general authorities from Utah. He laughed when Lorraine introduced him as the star of her aerobics class. During her stay in his area, she had led ward members in aerobics one night a week. When I asked how the building had been financed, he laughed and said, "Oh, the church forgave our debts. Imagine having your debts forgiven!"

Lorraine said that things seemed to be worse in Bacolad. Sister Balgos's baby, for instance, was three years old but didn't look a minute over six months. None of the children had grown in a year. She remarked that even though everyone seemed gaunter, their spirits were still strong. "They hide their sickness with laughter," she said.

## Iloilo

I was relieved when we boarded a boat for our trip to Iloilo, Lorraine's last assignment. We had first-class seats, but the main difference between us and the folks below decks was the privilege of watching the basketball game on television. Passengers on lower decks had to face in toward the boiler. The two-hour trip brought us to the lovely island of Panay. What a refreshing sight! It seemed to be covered with flowering trees. We could already see some of Lorraine's friends waving from the shore. "I can't believe it! How did they know what boat we would be on?" she cried. I was constantly surprised at the efficiency of informal communications networks in the Philippines. Hardly anybody owns a phone or a car, yet members seemed to be monitoring our every move. With the help of our welcoming committee, we checked into an American-style motel on a wide, tree-lined highway in the suburb of Molo. After freshening up, we hopped on a jeepney to find the Molo Ward, where all the members meet for Mutual and Institute on Saturday nights. The ward is a converted Spanish mansion also on a tree-lined drive. A lovely lady named Jessica, soon to depart for a mission to Hong Kong, was giving a lesson on "Sharing Your Talents." The young speaker who followed her was given the time signal by the bishop, who Lorraine said always wanted to move directly into games and talent sharing. In his spiffy white pants and black and white shirt, Bishop Elizan looked more than ready for the next event—dance lessons. A young man materialized from the crowd, introduced himself as Bobby, and tried unsuccessfully to teach me the cha-cha. This was only a pre-

lude to the main event—"Do You Love Your Neighbor," a form of musical chairs. "It" stands in the middle of the circle and picks someone
to answer the question, "Do you love your neighbor?"

"No!"

"Whom do you love?" with emphasis on whom. "I love everybody
with black hair."

"Everybody" then changes seats, and the one left must share a talent. Before the evening was out, I had performed an original dance,
and since mission rules forbid dancing, Lorraine, who never thought
she could sing, had performed a song in dialect. She was followed by a
farewell serenade from Sister Elizan, who sang to Lorraine through her
tears. I could certainly see why Iloilo has been christened "The City of
Love." After everyone had shared a talent, no matter how small, I was
asked to give the closing prayer.

Sunday morning, we went to the investigators' class, which was
taught by my dance instructor of the night before. Bobby, a young
man of about twenty-two, had served a mission in Manila, where he
had learned English and some fine teaching techniques. Using a combination of English, Ilongo, energetic gestures, and visual aids, he gave
a wonderful lesson on the apostasy.

I was once again called on to deliver the benediction, and we moved
into Relief Society, where I was chosen to offer the invocation. By then,
Lorraine and I had both been asked to speak in sacrament meeting.
Because conversations with Molo members revealed their envy of my
Mormon pioneer background and the fact that I was "born into the
church," I expressed envy of them and the joyous faith they had worked
so hard to maintain. "You chose to join the church," I said. "That took
courage. And it takes courage and faith to live its principles."

Lorraine's speech was a tearful goodbye, and the main speaker, a counselor in the bishopric, cried as he paid tribute to her missionary service.

The rest of the day was spent visiting the missionaries and members
in their homes. Some of them rode with us in the jeepneys and guided
us through beautiful landscapes of waving green rice. Lorraine tried to
sit on a carabao's back and was thrown into a small gunge ditch.

We met madonnas in sarongs holding young babies, older parents,
and grandparents like Lola, Bobby's grandmother, who lived in squat-

ter housing that she feared she must soon vacate. She earns a few pesos through sewing and embroidery. Lorraine's lavender dress was her handiwork. Bobby was planning to finish high school by taking an equivalency exam, but for now was, like most male Molo church members, out of work. He and two friends accompanied us on our visits, calling themselves "priesthood holders come to be your bodyguards." They went with us to the garden they had planted with the missionaries. They had also dug a well on the plot, and now enjoyed almost continuous harvests of bananas, corn, sweet potatoes, and coconut. "You just throw seeds and they grow!"

Bobby had picked a coconut from the garden that morning so his grandmother could serve us. When we reached her house, "young coconut" was waiting, and we could feel her excitement. She took a shy delight in showing us her handiwork, which included a blouse she was embroidering for Lorraine's going-away present.

Something about how she kept thinking of things to show us and to feed us reminded me of my youth and made me want to ask, "How did my mother get here—in Molo?"

This was not my only experience with déjà vu on this trip. That old cliché, "I must have known you in the pre-existence," kept coming to mind.

Our last stop took us across a veritable river of a gunge ditch. It was raining again, and the flimsy bamboo bridge was slippery. Bobby, walking backwards, took both my hands and guided me across. "We are very poor, Sister," he said.

"You are very courageous," I replied.

The next morning we spent four hours catching up with members we had missed the day before and packing the suitcases Lorraine had stored in the missionary apartment. One entire suitcase was filled with her journals. Fortunately, Bobby and the "priesthood holders" were again on hand to help. By the time we were ready, we had collected forty or fifty people, who either climbed on the jeepney with us or met us at the airport. Some of them pressed gifts into our hands. Sister Beng, a young woman of about twenty-two, and householp for the missionaries, had been with us almost the whole visit. A returned missionary herself, she declared that she was planning to serve another mission. She flexed her muscles and cried, "I am strong, and I can do anything!" This refreshing self-confidence was everywhere evident in the Molo ward.

At the airport, the priesthood holders asked Lorraine if they could kiss her. "Sorry," she said, "I'm still on my mission. You can kiss my mother, though!"

By the time we finally boarded the plane for Manila, everyone was sobbing. Our last sight was of their faces pushed against the fence at the runway. What was it about the experience that was making me feel that my whole life was about to change? Why did I find these people so hard to describe and so hard to leave? Everything I had been doing my whole life seemed suddenly irrelevant.

For eighteen months, Lorraine had been doing something important; it seemed that everything that she did helped in some way. I'll let her diary speak:

> Goodbye, my Molo family. Thank you for sharing the happiest months of my mission. It is in Molo that I learned who Jesus Christ really is and what it means to be a Christian. It is in Molo where I felt my testimony burn and become stable and beautiful. It is in Molo where I learned how to progress in suffering and how to deal with pain in a healthy way. It is in Molo where I learned to count my blessings. It is in Molo where I learned to love a life stripped of materialism and superficiality.
>
> My mission was more than just an "experience" that can be learned from and "applied." I don't want to adjust to a materialistic, "Me" society. I want to be pure and real. I want to sing from my heart and dance from my spirit. I want to live on rice, the Book of Mormon, and laughter. I want to have total faith in God during affliction. I want to catch cockroaches and giggle. I want to collect shells for abstracts on the beach. I want to sit at the top of the coconut tree and eat guava and mango.

In Manila, we stayed at a Holiday Inn that Chick had arranged for us. After eating soup in the coffee shop, Lorraine burst into tears. "That soup cost enough to feed a family for a whole week!"

Our last hurdle was the Manila airport. After wrestling our heavy bags through the check-in counter, we stood there feeling dazed. "Where are the priesthood holders now that we need them?" Almost immediately a young man introduced himself as a high priest in the Manila Stake and an employee of the airport. He offered to guide us through immigration and customs. We had forgotten all about immigration and customs. Lorraine's name tag had saved us again.

Now, as I try to process my mission experience, I look at a shell ornament that sits on my desk, a gift from Sister Beng in Iloilo. She had carefully painted a coconut tree and a figure that looks strangely like me in my red shirt and green pants balanced precariously on a bridge. Inscribed below is the scripture, "Trust in the Lord with all thine heart and lean not unto thine own understanding. In all thy ways, acknowledge him and he shall direct thy path."

Thanks, my Philippine brothers and sisters. I needed that.

[1985]

# A TEN-DAY
# EXPERT SPEAKS

Shortly after Lorraine and I returned from her mission, we, like the rest of the world, witnessed on television the dramatic Philippine revolution led by Corazon Aquino. The editors of *Exponent II* asked me what we were thinking about the new woman president and what we were hearing from our friends in the Philippines.

Even a ten-day expert can see that Corazon Aquino is no ordinary politician. A well-educated woman of "good" family who went to school in Westchester County, New York, she married into another good family. Like many women, she put her own ambitions on the back burner while rearing her children and supporting her husband's career. Her quiet, competent manner was considered proper for the wife of an ambitious military man. But with the death of her husband, Benigno "Ninoy" Aquino, his supporters looked to her, and her political energies were released. Rich and poor alike, armed with flowers and prayers, flooded the streets, proving once and for all the strengh of numbers. As they stood against tanks and soldiers, like the stripling warriors in the Book of Mormon, they presented an impregnable force. After the peaceful revolt and her assumption of power, Aquino surrounded herself with experienced people including some of her exiled countrymen and women who had fled the Marcos regime.

She and her people are presenting the world with an experiment in democracy, in Christianity, if you will. First, she sought no revenge on the murderers of her husband except to promise them lawful trials. Although other politicians have faulted her for naiveté and her own brand of cronyism, she opened the prisons, shook hands with the Communists, and invited them to talk. She has put down several coup attempts and is attempting to hold a free election. The world waits breathlessly to see how this country, once tutored by the United States, will go about reclaiming their land under this soft-spoken woman. In his abortive presidential campaign, Joseph Smith recommended opening the prisons: "Petition your state legislature to pardon every convict in their several penitentiaries; blessing them as they go, and saying to them in the name of the Lord, go thy way and sin no more."

A question we heard is whether women rulers would be more inclined than men to achieve peace. Susa Young Gates, an early Mormon heroine, thought not. "Women often make the mistake of urging that the vote will help them to purify politics and reform the world. What nonsense!" I feel that as more women come into power, discussion about their abilities will center on their individual competence and not on their gender.

One friend remarked that Golda Meir's grandmotherly qualities contributed to her effectiveness. Consumer advocate Esther Peterson has irked business and government leaders, especially in her work with third-world countries. "You can't be nanny to the whole world, Esther!" one admonished her. But she laughed and took it as a compliment. "I could try!" she said.

After Lorraine's mission call two years ago, I went to our ancient encyclopedia to look up the unfamiliar word "Cebu." I learned that the Philippines has traditionally favored equality for women, partly because its earliest tribes were matriarchal. The influence of the Spanish and the Moslems weakened women's rights, but American influence brought co-education and women's suffrage to the islands. During my trip, I noticed that poverty seemed to upgrade the status of women. Women who can cook, sew, and perform other domestic labors can often find work when men cannot.

My encyclopedia also reported that the Philippines was once one of the world's leading growers of rice, sugar cane, fruit, and copra (coconut products). The road system, built by the U.S., was the best in Asia. And the large islands of Negros and Panay, part of Lorraine's mission, were fertile and hospitable to growth and industry. Yet today the Philippines is not prospering. The dictatorial feudal system created by Marcos has rendered the land inaccessible to most of its people. Land reform is one of Aquino's greatest challenges.

The Philippines' finest natural resource is its people. Family-oriented and quick to learn, they are now in dire need of food, education, and housing. The people of the Cebu Mission are constantly rebuilding their falling huts and saving what few pennies they make for their children's education. No Relief Society sister ever made so much from so little as Sister Abajo of Cebu City. She writes that she is still holding missionary lessons in her home, crocheting jeepney decorations, and rebuilding her hut after each typhoon.

I think of the Valencia Mormons whose destitution has driven their mothers to domestic servitude in prosperous Singapore. I see the family of Bishop Santillan of the Mormon compound in Bacolad who paints pictures and teaches his children to sing Utah hymns. His wife writes that the folks in the compound are learning "self-reliance," a missionary welfare program teaching cleanliness that is meant to fight the effects of the gunge ditch. She adds her gratitude for a church that "teaches us to develop our talents." Her husband's art is "one source of our livelihood." She says that she believes "keeping the commandments" will keep her country out of civil war.

I think of Erkie, the energetic ward mission leader in Tanjay, who is scheduled to leave Joann and the baby for a job in Kuwait. I see Lola and Bobby eking out a living in their squatter housing. They write that the church is building a chapel on the Molo garden that feeds them and the other Mormons nearby. This was the garden with the clean-water well that Lorraine and the welfare missionaries helped plant. How will the people eat now?

The ascendancy of Aquino gave them hope. Always afraid to discuss politics, our friends now write of the day Marcos left the country: "We had thought last Tuesday that there was a war already because of the sounds of armiture [sic], but it was a different kind of firearms. Now since the time that Marcos has left, the people have been merry making. This was like the new year and I could see the happiness of the people who were dancing and singing in the streets."

Somewhat apprehensively, I had sent copies of *Exponent II* to some of Lorraine's friends in the mission, wondering what they would think of my account of my ten-day mission among them. Bobby wrote back: "I read it when I was about to sleep, and WOW! Honestly, Nanay Mary, I love very much reading it. It was a beautiful and uplifting story."

Bobby is part of a group of young men who are unusually proud of priesthood designations, like elder and high priest, but they see their offices as a call to service. "We are the priesthood holders come to carry your bags." They would help us through customs or onto the right bus, whatever was needed. In the Book of Mormon, Helaman's sons were described as "all young men exceedingly valiant for courage, and also for strength and activity; but behold, this was not all, they were men who were true at all times in whatsoever thing they were entrusted" (Alma 53:20).

Meanwhile, Bobby's grandmother writes that her hut has once more been hit by wind and rain. "I am in very good health. But I have a very big problem with my house. It's about to fall." With typhoon season not far off, she and Bobby are at risk.

Just as I was about to send money for the house (it would cost about thirty-five American dollars to rebuild the hut), another letter came from Bobby: "I am glad to tell you that we are starting to repair our house. We received a small amount from the church, which I combined with savings from my bamboo bank." One of the bamboo posts that hold up the house inside his "humble room" has a hole "in which a peso can enter." He has been depositing his change in the bamboo bank to be used for a trip to the temple in Manila. Last year he used the money to rebuild the house. After adding to the fund by taking the bus to work instead of a jeepney, he has once again spent it on bamboo for the house.

I store our family's unwanted pennies in a small purse in a kitchen drawer. Once I counted them and took them to the bank. The teller was not glad to see me, so I have let them pile up again. I think I'll see if I can deposit them in Bobby's bank by adding them to the money order that I am going to send.

"Our house is quite beautiful," Bobby reports. "The materials we used are the most cheapest materials in which we can afford to buy, but I can be proud of it when it is finished."

[1986]

# AS WE RODE OUT ONE LATE SUMMER MORNING

When my eldest son Stephen called from L.A. to say he was planning a sentimental journey to his mission field—Madrid, Spain—I tried to talk him out of it. He countered with, "More people die in their bathtubs than in terrorist attacks." He also said he would find a cheap charter to Paris and a cheap rental car. Most law clerks take a trip "abroad" between the bar exam and serious work at their new jobs.

"And, Mom, I want you to go with me. After all, you've seen Lorraine's and Scott's missions, why not mine?"

My fears of terrorism subsided. "Why not?" I thought. Our family had planned to meet Steve in Spain at the end of his mission in 1980, but Steve had decided he didn't want us to come. He was tired and ready to come home. So Steve came from L.A. and we each packed a single overnight bag. This was no easy task for one whose luggage makes strong men cry, but I wanted to take only what would fit under the airplane seat.

Rental cars are cheaper in Paris, so Steve arranged for a brand new Citroen. In fact, he picked it up at the factory across town. Not speaking French, he asked no questions. He simply got in and drove back to our hotel with an unfamiliar stick shift that poked straight out from the dashboard. I think it amazing that a son of mine could find his way around a foreign city in a strange car, but he is Chick's son, too, and Chick is an amazing bird dog.

For some reason the little golden Citroen looked like an art deco version of my Dad's '28 Chevy. The two-door, four-seater with a rollback top seemed just right for the two of us and our luggage.

We stopped in Chartres in deference to my reading of Henry Adams's account of it in college. I was convinced that the Chartres Cathedral was a must for any educated woman. Steve assured me, however, that the cathedrals in Spain were far superior to any in France and that our best bet was to find them *toute suite!* So we barreled on through France on a smooth highway that cut through remarkably beautiful farm country. I was impressed by the clean rest stops where you could get omelettes cooked in a flash and served with fresh croissants, but Steve would hear no praise of France. Someone had tried to cheat him at the last gas station, and he couldn't wait to reach familiar ground where people were honest.

We stopped for the night at Tours, awakened early to a driving rain, watched the open landscape change gradually into Gascoyne Forest, and finally showed our passports through closed windows at San Sebastian in the Pyrenees—Basque country. I expected soldiers and bayonets and other signs of anti-terrorism, but I saw only mountains and bilingual road signs. One language was obviously Spanish, but the other language had x's and z's in odd places. The Basques feel they are an entirely different people, said Stephen. They claim their language is the original Adamic and want to secede from Spain.

The peaks of the Pyrenees reached up through clouds of rain and our jitney climbed to meet them. We were shrouded in mist as we descended, then the landscape changed suddenly to southern Utah. A winding dirt road brought us to our first *parador*, which is a state-sponsored hotel on a historic site. We were in Vitoria checking into the former home of the duke who had helped found the city in the 1500s. Our whitewashed room opened onto purple hills and the ghostly remains of an ancient village.

"We made it, Mom! I can't believe we're actually here!" I had been thinking how much he had always loved traveling. In fact, his first trip was in our convertible from Utah to Virginia in sub-zero weather when he was six weeks old. The car froze up every time we stopped, and Stephen just ate, slept, and smiled. At a service station somewhere in the Midwest, Chick fell out of the car with Steve on his belly. Not a peep out of Steve—he enjoyed that ride too! When Steve was a lively two, our doctor warned us that taking him cross-country in a car would drive us all crazy. But Steve sang and chortled as he gazed at the scenery from the back of our station wagon.

Steve takes after his father in his devotion to travel. Before I met Chick, I was a timid traveler, the kind who is glad she went after she gets home but doesn't look forward to going again. Chick changed all that. Three months after our wedding, we moved from Utah to Arlington, Virginia, and he has acted as unofficial tour guide ever since. Now Steve was my tour guide. Armed with a student guide book, a Spanish dictionary, letters from Spanish converts, and his missionary diary, he had planned a two-week itinerary that would take us to the cities of his mission and nearby landmarks. Besides making some reservations, we had prepared ourselves by reading Laurie Lee's poetic autobiography, *As I Walked Out One Midsummer Morning*. Lee had left his village in the Cotswolds in 1934 when he was nineteen years old. He walked down through England and took a ship to Spain in his first experience with a foreign country. It was a coming of age for him. He explored Spain, fell in love with it, and sneaked out just ahead of the Spanish civil war.

Stephen, too, was nineteen when he went to Spain. In a way, his trip was a Mormon boy's coming of age. But Lee was cutting his cords, leaving family behind to be completely on his own, free to observe, to beg, to sleep out of doors, to risk injury and illness, to live by his wits. Lee's was a romantic journey, the passage of a young poet. Steve, on the other hand, was fulfilling the dreams of others according to a pattern of expectation, part of a world-wide army, never to be alone, except briefly and accidentally.

Lee awoke in the hull of a ship knowing that he was beginning a new life with a "few shillings in my pocket and no return ticket." Steve knew his tour was proscribed, that he would be sent wherever and whenever his leaders decided, that he would be expected to discipline himself and others, that he would be expected to teach strangers at short notice, trusting in God for his safety.

Lee arrived in Spain with a "knapsack, blanket, spare shirt, and a fiddle, and enough words to ask for a glass of water." Stephen arrived with two suitcases, his scriptures, money enough to keep him for the first month, and memorized lessons crammed into his head at a two-month training session. He had always valued privacy, his own room, his own car, and the ability to fend for himself, but he was surprisingly happy within his new limitations. The mission was delaying the necessity of choosing a wife and a career.

At the time, 1978, the Madrid mission included central and northwestern Spain, where the missionaries lived only in cities and suburbs and were not allowed to drive cars or ride bikes.

While Lee described his first taste of Spain as "cold and dim, an unlighted ruin, smothered in the dead blue dusk," Stephen was introduced to a lively country that was recovering from Franco's forty-year rule and slowly changing itself into a democracy. It was also a Catholic country that had only recently opened to missionaries from other faiths. Steve's first year was served under a mission president who allowed the missionaries to sightsee one day a week, enabling him to visit the Prado, Toledo, Segovia, and the beach. In his second year, a new president clamped down on the sightseeing, requiring the missionaries to wear their suits even on their "P" Days.

The mission had not included Vitoria, so the next morning, we left for Valladolid, which had been his first assignment. On the way was the ancient city of Burgos, with its legendary gate and pure Gothic cathedral and polychrome sculpture. Stephen described his shock at first seeing the crucified Christ in living color, hanging from the cross in cowhide and real hair. "I thought I had truly entered the land of the 'great and abominable church.'" But now he was thrilled at entering a city that had been founded back in the ninth century. It had been the capital of Old Castile, the birthplace of the pure Castilian language that Steve was so proud of. It was also the burial place of El Cid and Franco.

It was here that I had my first taste of a Spanish tortilla sandwich—potatoes and scrambled egg between two large hunks of white roll. "How is it?" Steve asked eagerly.

"Well," I said, "is there some ketchup?"

"Mother! Are you crazy?" he cried. "You won't serve ketchup at home and now you want to put it on Spain's best-loved dish?" I apologized and vowed to like the best-loved dish.

On the way to Valladolid, we remembered that Laurie Lee's first impression of the city was not a happy one: "A dark, square city, hard as its syllables—a shut box, full of the pious dust and preserved breath of its dead. . . . A city of expired fanaticisms and murdered adorations—

of the delicate and elaborate Moors, of Ferdinand and Isabella, of the deceived Columbus, and the gentle, crisp-brained Cervantes."

Though our approach was sunnier and more cheerful than Lee's had been, Steve's first reaction was surprise. The medium-sized city he remembered had become a big city surrounded and extended by tall, orange apartment buildings and bewildering highways. "Everybody's more prosperous," he said, noting the cranes and bulldozers along the teeming highway. The center city, where he hoped to find the church and his former apartment, had become a maze of one-way streets. We did finally find the apartment, sandwiched inside a large development with a square of small shops in the middle. It no longer housed the missionaries, nor did the new owner of Steve's favorite fruit stand remember any "Mormones."

A bit downhearted, we searched for the Mormon chapel, and after many twistings and turnings, located it, only to be told that the Mormons had moved, nobody knew where.

We were heartened to find, however, the Colon Museo, supposedly the reconstructed home where Christopher Columbus had breathed his last. But we failed to find Cervantes's home, circling until our car began to sputter and stall. The locals were more than happy to direct us, especially since Steve could speak their language, but the directions never panned out. In desperation, we decided to stop for gas and to hit the road for Avila. We didn't anoint the car but did say a little prayer when the gas station attendant looked under the hood and pronounced the engine so dirty that it needed to be repaired by his colleague up the street. Reasoning that a newly minted car couldn't be that dirty, we decided to drive off. From that moment, the car ran without a minute's trouble.

Steve was morose until we were through the rush and out into the colorful plains. A parador waited for us in the walled city of Avila, on a high plateau in the Sierra de Gredos Mountains. To get to it, we crossed land that was obviously being reclaimed. Fields of shorn wheat alternated with those of sunflowers and grape vines. Sprinklers were everywhere. On the river and in the mountains, dams and reservoirs stored water for energy and planting. And every few miles a village announced itself with church towers outlined against the orange and gold sky. Between villages were the walkers, sometimes solitary, sometimes in groups. The men invariably wore black or blue berets and folded their arms behind their backs. Women were usually swinging sticks or branches and chatting with other women. Most of Spain walks out after dinner. In this case, they seemed to be headed for villages at least fifteen to twenty miles away. The lingering sunset lit up their paths in kaleidoscopic colors. We arrived at Avila just as its serpentine walls turned white in the failing light. A stork's nest guarded the massive entry gate. Our parador, just inside the gate, was the former palace of Duke Raimundo de Borgona, who won Avila from the Moors in the fifteenth century and erected the stone wall for protection. With eighty-eight towers and nine gateways, it is a masterpiece.

As soon as we had checked in, we went back outside to climb the wall for a look at the surrounding countryside. I had reached the walkway on the top when I was stricken with vertigo and had to be helped back down. How embarrassing. I admired the roses in the garden, while Steve climbed to the top of the tower.

The next day we wandered all over the fascinating little city and paid court to the spirit of Santa Teresa, the intellectual nun. Her birth place and convent stand together and a large white statue of her guards the cathedral.

During our two nights in Avila, Steve read to me from his diary: "Everyone in Spain loves to just *pasear* or go out and take walks. For example, almost every late night that I've been teaching at José Gutierrez's house, his two kids will finish up their homework around ten, will pop their heads in the room and each will say, '*me voy.*' Then they'll go walking for about forty-five minutes. I think it's their way of clearing their heads after studying for so long. Spain is great!"

His diary also tells of his eagerness to learn the language well enough to joke with the people, to use his personality in introducing the gospel. As he reread the passages, he laughed at his egoism. "I actually thought everything depended on me. That if I could just be worthy, the people would get baptized with practically no work on their part!" He saw how easily he had forgotten the "free agency" of the people he was trying to teach.

"Well, you were trained that way," I responded.

"I'm glad I went on a mission," he continued. "It forced me to discover my spiritual self and develop a testimony of the gospel. It also kept me from getting engaged to the wrong girl. Believing that it all depended on my personal worthiness may have been a misconception, but as an egotistical nineteen-year-old, I may not have stuck with it otherwise."

The next morning on our way to Toledo, I asked him what he thought about the constant pressure to baptize. His diary made it sound as if the act itself were all that mattered.

"I gotta baptize!" he wrote. "I want to get them wet by next month"—referring to a family he was teaching, and when, saints be praised, they did get wet, he would fill a whole page with the words, "I *baptized!*"

"Unfortunately, success in the mission field is equated with numbers of baptisms. I do think part of my interest in baptism came from a desire to succeed at whatever I was doing, but I really wanted to make people's lives better."

We were now approaching the city I had wanted to see more than any other, the adopted home and the inspiration of that glorious mystic, El Greco. Imagine a city that began with the Romans in 192, was conquered by the Visigoths, who were defeated by the Moors, who ruled for three hundred years, and then was finally "reconquered" by the Christian king of Spain in 1085! As Fodor's guide book puts it, "Toledo is a museum of the Spanish spirit, both inside and out." Built on high rock clusters, the whole city is like a walled medieval castle guarded by its moat—the river Tagus.

I had been warned that Toledo was a tourist trap, but I didn't care. That night we chose to stay across the river on a hill facing the city. Our modern *parador* stood on the site of the villa of the Duke of Orgaz, the same Orgaz in the El Greco painting that is so precious it hangs in its own chapel not far from his tomb.

After checking in, we returned to Toledo and parked our car just inside the wall. Beginning with El Greco's grave, we worked our way up the hill on foot to the cathedral. Buildings on the steep, narrow streets of Toledo seemed to be leaning against each other in such a crowded way that I was inside the cathedral before I had really seen it. Then I felt completely dwarfed and overawed, as I was by so much of Spain. This edifice was so tall that I almost fell backwards trying to see the tops of its interior pillars. Separate tickets were sold for each of the many treasure rooms. Since it would take weeks to see them all, we chose the room containing El Greco paintings, including his mighty apostle series. As a bonus, there hung a wonderful painting of Christ by Goya.

After staggering out of the cathedral, we pointed ourselves toward the Alcazar, a large square palace across town that had been the scene of the Republican surrender during the civil war. It had been a dungeon, a hospital, a hideout, then an office for Franco's men. Dreary, cold, and dank, it brought unwelcome thoughts of war. We were huppy to leave it and to search out the Santa Cruz Museum, formerly a hospital. Gregorian chants set the mood for medieval art treasures and twenty-two more paintings by El Greco. A magnificent drapery, with what appeared to be a tie-dyed image of Christ, hung from the cruciform ceiling. It was the sail from the ship Cervantes had sailed during the ill-fated battle of Lepanto.

I soon felt stuffed with art, glutted, my eyes burning with beauty. I wasn't even annoyed by the shops full of cheap trinkets. Toledo was all I had expected and more.

At the *parador*, I watched the sunset while Steve swam in the pool just below our balcony. A perfect evening! When he came in, we planned the next phase of our trip to La Mancha and thence to Madrid.

To prepare for Madrid, where Steve had spent six months, we read again from his journal: "I feel like the Lord may have a special calling for me as a missionary to bring older people into the gospel. I've always been able to understand and get along with older people throughout my life. When I first arrived in the mission field, I baptized a 57-year-old woman and a married couple of 60-plus years. Today I knocked on the door of an older couple who have gone through much suffering in their lives; they want to believe that God loves them, but they're not sure anymore. We taught a *charla* and then we all knelt down, so I could use my priesthood authority to leave a blessing in their home. I raised my right arm to the square and pronounced the blessing, and the spirit was very strong. As we got up, there were tears in their eyes, and they were smiling."

I knew he was hoping to find one of his beloved "older" converts, Maria, who had reverted to her native Catholicism after his release. She had written her reasons: "I saw you as an angel from God. When you left, my revelation left. The ones who came next didn't measure up." This was a blow for the branch since she had been zealous in her work there. "The pull was too strong," Steve said. "She is a visionary person, and she believes God has called her back to Catholicism."

As soon as we departed from Toledo, I opened our paperback copy of *Don Quixote,* another visionary, older person. Once we got through the smaller cities and out onto the open plains, it was not difficult to imagine the ancient knight, his pitiful horse, and his trusty companion. Even though most of the windmills seemed to have been replaced by transformers, we could see whitewashed windmills in the distance.

Hours of dusty driving brought us to Campo de Criptana, a town of windmills. It was siesta time, so there were no stores open where we might quench our thirst. We struggled up the central hill to eight windmills that are part of a monument to Cervantes. One, ancient and broken-down, housed a small postcard shop, while the other windmills looked suspiciously new and clean. All had their arms bound. Of course, that didn't keep us from snapping pictures of each other in the bright wind that whipped at our hair and clothes.

Our next stop was El Toboso, a town that chose to play the part of Dulcinea's home. It, too, resembled a ghost town, but Steve assured me that lovely homes lurked behind the locked gates and white walls. We wound around until we found the central plaza with its colorful city hall and scrap-iron sculpture of the doleful knight and his sturdy lady. We were then able to follow quotations from the text of *Don Quixote* that were painted on walls leading to a reproduction of the sixteenth century "palace" of Dulcinea.

After leaving La Mancha, we pondered the windmill-jousting we Mormons do when we send our children to ancient lands armed with the conviction that they can change the lives of the people. I felt cowed by Spain, such a solid country, with power deep in its bones, a massive presence. Stephen and I talked of the naiveté with which the missionaries judge what they see.

That evening, we entered the suburbs of Madrid, which had doubled in size since Stephen's day. Tall and identical apartment buildings formed a deepening wall around the city. Alcorcon was now dwarfed by newer developments. None of Stephen's friends were home, so we decided to drive into the city. Since tomorrow was Sunday, we could come back for church.

After getting lost several times, we found a highrise Holiday Inn on a busy, glittering avenue. The next morning, I felt dwarfed again. From the roof of our hotel, the city extended to the distant Guardarama Mountains under a clear, sunny sky. This city of wide avenues and heroic buildings sprawled to at least twice the size of Washington, D.C.

On the way to the Madrid Ward, I asked Steve how he would feel if he were to find that most of his converts had slid away. He said he would be disappointed but that "when people make an enormous decision to change their lives, it doesn't always work out. Some can't live by pure ideal. Sometimes the programs are not in place for them. They leave what they know to join with thirty or forty people who may be meeting in a basement, and they're bored."

"So, is it worth it?"

"Well, even if they leave, they have learned important things and they're better for it. Some experience a kind of catharsis. Some have never really thought about spiritual matters before, and they benefit."

We attended two meetings that day, and in both there was a warm welcome for Steve and a chance to visit with converts. We checked out of the Holiday Inn the next morning and went blithely off to a little town in the foothills of the Guardarama Mountains to see the bullfights. Taking time for a drive, we gazed at bull ranches and the glorious Manzanares Castle. Hemingway's *For Whom the Bell Tolls* was set in these mountains where Franco had won some bloody battles with Republican guerrillas. We breathed deeply of the pines that grew thickly all the way up to the lodge at the top.

Then back down to the bullfights—six, twenty-minute events with three matadors. One of the matadors was his own picador and his own worst enemy. He "picked" the bull so well that the poor thing couldn't fight well enough to challenge the matador's glory. The bull died right in front of our front row seat. As I stared at the blood and the sneer on the young matador's face, Steve reminded me that bullfighting is not a sport, but an art.

Returning to Madrid at ten, exhausted and without a room, we relied on our guide book and were led to an address on Princess Street near the university. We knocked at the heavy iron gate that obscured the door to the building, and when no answer came, went into a bar where Steve made a call to the innkeeper who said his hotel was full but he would rescue us anyway. Apprehensive about what that might mean, we agreed. When he finally opened the door, we were led to an elevator that took us to the fifth floor, half of which was his small "hostal."

We sat down with two other guests, who were watching *Miami Vice* on television. Our host, stationing himself at his ironing board, talked nonstop about American movie stars. Stephen laughed and translated from time to time while I tried not to snore. Finally, the two men excused themselves, and our host folded up the ironing board, which turned out to be a cover for two roll-away beds. After draping a small, ruffled curtain over the television screen, he made the beds, pointed out the bathroom down the hall, and bade us goodnight.

In Iberia, Michener marvels that "the taciturn Spaniard of history could make so much noise." That night we learned just how much noise the Spaniards could make and how much we could take. Because of the hot night, we had left the window open. The noise washed over us, in us, never subsiding, only adding layers of new sound as the night wore on.

The next morning, after a breakfast of chocolate with "churros" that hit our stomachs like lead, we met José Luis from the Alcorcon Branch, who had offered to guide us through the Goya, the El Greco, and the Velasquez displays in the Prado. I was struck with José Luis's eyes, black with points of light in the centers, much like the eyes of El Greco's saints. "From my Moorish ancestors," he said. In a few hours, we were reeling with the great gulps of art we were taking in. After we saw Picasso's *Guernica* in a museum across the street, José Luis left us.

We started our walking tour of Madrid at nearby Retiro Park, a green paradise of 400 acres in the center of the city. Cutting through a corner of it, we were on our way to the Plaza Mayor, the Plaza del Sol, and the Plaza Español. Madrid is the heart of Spain, and we were in the heart of Madrid. We were also in the heart of Steve's mission and near the ancient apartments where he had lived as zone leader. These apartments date from the seventeenth century and are a stone's throw from the royal palace.

Steve recited some Spanish history and pointed out that the Plaza del Sol was the setting for Goya's *Seventh of May.* At the Plaza Mayor we sat down at an outdoor cafe while Steve fantasized about renting an apartment there for a year or so. I could see why he would like that. The Spanish people, the Spanish landscape, the Spanish skies seemed enough inspiration to last a lifetime. I used to believe that El Greco's work was drawn mostly from his mystical, feverish imagination, but now I have seen part of what he saw, and I know he also drew from the fecund life around him.

As we rested by the statues of Cervantes and his creations in the Plaza Espanol, I said I could understand why Steve was disappointed at his transfer from there to the far northwest corner of Spain. After serving as a zone leader and working hard to line up baptisms, he was sent away for the last three months of his mission. It was to relatively slow and backward Galicia, a province of coal mining, shipbuilding, and small arms manufacture.

We finally reached our car and the road to Segovia, our next stop. Steve allowed that the country seemed more prosperous, more sophisticated, less religious than when he was here before. "I guess that's what democracy does for you."

The entrance to Segovia is at the famous Roman aqueduct rising to a height of a hundred feet. Stephen had sent pictures from his mission showing him atop it in a "Samuel the Lamanite" pose. We examined the brick work, made without mortar by the Romans, each stone carved to fit. Amazing! Behind it the city rose on a pile of apricot-colored rock in the shape of a ship whose prow was the elegant castle used in the movie *Camelot.* Our *parador* was a new building, clinging to the cliffs across from the castle. We were given two bedrooms and a bath down a long hall.

The next morning, we climbed the castle on narrow, circular stone steps inside one of the massive towers. Steve called encouragement from ahead, while I puffed to the top without the vertigo I had experienced in Avila. Tramping around Spain was toughening me up. As we left Segovia and began two long days that would end in La Coruna, we watched the landscape change from rocky mountains with pine trees to soft, green farmland very close to the ocean, hazy and poetic, like Wales. The scenery was restful to the eyes and the mind, and I soon understood why Stephen, so reluctant to leave Madrid, had come to accept La Coruna as his favorite spot.

His diary records that his first impression was not hopeful. Knocking on doors in a crowded seatown was unfruitful, even frightening. Baptisms had been few, and he couldn't see how he could do much during the final weeks of his mission. By the time he was adjusted, it would be time to leave.

But he soon responded to the friendliness of the members and the challenge of his job as district leader and zone leader. His responsibilities were visiting bank presidents in their offices and dock workers down by the ships. He also set up board displays in the center of the city. This brought many investigators. One of these was a shy young man called Melchor, who came with two boisterous friends. He didn't seem "golden" at first, and when Steve baptized him, he seemed happy though not overjoyed. Melchor had been on the verge of backing out, and Steve was not sure he would find the courage to stay with the church. His people, direct descendants of ancient Celtic tribes, still speak an archaic language, and he had not learned Spanish until he started school at age nine. He wrote Steve that he was still faithful, and he invited us to stay with him, his wife, and their three-month-old son "Esteban," named for Stephen.

It is a good thing that the Spanish day is long. It was four in the afternoon when we found our little family, tucked away in a second floor apartment in a decaying part of town. After exclaiming over Steve's namesake, who had inherited his father's Celtic eyes, and being won over by Marisa, an intelligent school teacher who didn't speak much English but was very eloquent with her hands, we sat down to a robust meal of veal, eggs, potatoes, and cocoa. Then we went sightseeing to the nearby Hercules Tower, a lighthouse from Roman times that overlooks the ocean and the busy seaport; to the central city where we lost ourselves in a bookstall that covered the length of the square; to an ancient castle, now a museum of prehistoric celtic artifacts.

At ten o'clock we went back to the apartment to be served another complete meal!

Melchor talked the whole time, with Stephen translating. We learned he had served a mission and on his return was unable to find a job. Finally, the church hired him to microfilm Catholic genealogy records and he was able to marry Marisa. Her family had been generous in helping the couple, and they were comfortable in their tiny three-room apartment.

At one point during their reminiscences, Steve said, "I think I may have baptized a couple of people I shouldn't have. One didn't understand the gospel and one wasn't ready." Melchor replied, "Our Heavenly Father wants all his children to be baptized." I was touched by the simplicity of his faith. Sometimes, I even envy it.

The next day we began a long and winding trip along the northern coast, stopping at fishing villages and a *parador* in the city of Gijon. Reaching our approximate entry point in the Pyrenees of almost two weeks before, Steve left me on the train to Paris. He would spend two more weeks in Spain, where he would speak to the La Coruna branch and visit Maria in Alcorcon. I had seen less than half of Spain and my appetite was whetted for more.

Stephen had recorded in his diary his thoughts at leaving the mission field: "The mission represents our earthly testing experience. We left the security of our homes and families to be tested here. If we have served faithful and honorable missions, our reunion with our parents and loved ones will be truly joyful. So it is with life. If we remain true and faithful to the end, we will be received with joy by our Heavenly Parents." More than a sightseeing tour, my trip with Stephen had allowed me to see his growth and know him better as a man. He has always gone forth with an uncanny ability to project himself into the future. I believe in that future, and I am grateful that he has become my friend and confidant.

I no longer feel guilty about our naiveté as travelers and missionaries. Every "first time" is naive. In a way, everything that happens is for the first time.

[1986]

# V
## Hanging On

# SUDDENLY SINGLE

As I sit here in my new condo, I am aware I am living alone for the first time in my life. I am even more aware that I am alone in my body. Painfully aware. The bones that never quite healed are speaking to me along with the heart that lies in pieces. (How self-serving and sentimental that sounds!) I wish I had taken better care of my body—my bone house, as the Anglo-Saxon poets called it. The aches and pains I find easy to ignore in company seem urgent when nobody is around. I know I will do nothing about them, however, except take Ibuprofen and think more dark thoughts.

I wanted this condo, I tell myself. I needed to slim down in every way. My beloved home of thirty years had become a money pit. It was time to distribute my collections among my children. I took some pleasure in giving the piano to my daughter and her budding musicians. I felt virtuous as I asked my grandchildren to choose from my precious souvenirs. I thought I could hear the voice of my deceased economist husband congratulating me on finally making prudent accounting decisions. I felt good about dispersing my not inconsiderable library. "I've read most of them," I tell myself. "Somebody else can enjoy them now."

The house sale went so smoothly, it didn't even go on the market. I closed on house and condo the same day. The condo had been owned by people of good taste. They had decorated in my own colors, had laid down non-allergenic carpeting, and, Praise be! had added built-in shelves to every room.

Unfortunately, after everything was put away, I realized that a hole had opened in my heart, a hole where my library used to be. Many favorites survived, volumes from my childhood, classics from my college days, books written by me, my family, and friends, and references I need for future writing projects. But I couldn't help myself, I went into mourning for the rest.

"You can buy new ones!" a friend tells me. "Besides, everything is on the internet anyway." I respond that my books were my personal history, my consolation, my companions. I don't really believe everything is on the internet, and what's more, I'm not ready to replace the heft, the scent, the portability of a book with a cold electronic screen.

But then, I am a relic of a bygone age. If I were not, would I be sitting alone in a retirement condo? A thought comes to me from one of the classics I saved:

> Word I was in the house alone
> Somehow must have gotten abroad,
> Word I had no one left but God.[1]

As the bleak definition of aloneness and the irony of that last line reach my heart, my Mormon upbringing reminds me that with God I am never truly alone.

What then is the difference between alone and loneliness? I put this question to a philosophically inclined friend: "Alone," she said, "is a welcome state for creative people. Loneliness is selfish, self-pitying, and devoutly to be avoided."

In my busiest years as a young mother, I often dreamed of being alone—absolutely alone in a white cell with a view of trees. A longing built up within me of a need for space. More space could bring submerged poetry to the surface, and the writer I was meant to be could emerge. On our family's trip to Europe with another family, I often felt the urge to leave the lively group. As we drove through the streets of Paris, I actually had to fight the temptation to open the door and disappear down a side street.

As the children grew older and our house expanded, I managed to create an office where I could retreat for a few hours a day. I worked out a routine whereby I devoted attention to my projects while others worked on theirs. Concentration came more quickly when others were working. This is how I maintained the editorship and publication of *Dialogue* from the family basement. I had found a way to be creatively alone.

Now it seems that my long-ago wish for a clean, well-lighted cell has been granted. I have only my best-loved objects surrounding me. My new office has a built-in computer desk and good light. There is a tree-filled window. I need not venture out in the Code Red air; a deli on the premises delivers lunch and my daughter is fifteen minutes away. Finally, my creative life can blossom, my neglected projects bloom!

It is very quiet here, unlike apartments I lived in years ago. An extra layer of masonry protects me from the neighbor's plumbing. Another neighbor calls it as "quiet as a tomb," which resurrects a line from Andrew Marvell's "To His Coy Mistress": "The grave's a fine and private place / But none, I think, do there embrace."

This nest, so perfect for my streamlined belongings, is not just quiet, it is small. Where are the cathedral ceilings from that hospitable manor once dubbed "the Bradford motel" by the folk who stayed with us? And where is the extra bed for just one more guest? I am not just alone, I tell myself. I am lonely.

I think of friends in Ireland who used *lonely* to describe their feelings when a beloved priest was transferred. Some could not bring themselves to attend his farewell party. "I would feel too lonely," they said. An Irish friend, seeing me off at the airport, admonished me, "Now don't be lonely." I translate that to mean "Try not to miss me too much!"

In his Nobel acceptance speech, Octavio Paz spoke of the "consciousness of being separate" as "a constant feature of our *spiritual* history." I am intrigued by the way he located this condition as part of our spiritual history. He goes on to say that

> this separation is sometimes experienced as a wound that marks an internal division, an anguished awareness that invites introspection; at other times it appears as a challenge, a spur to action, to go forth into the outside world and encounter others. It is true that the feeling of separation is universal. . . . It is born at the very moment of our birth; as we are wrenched from the Whole, we fall into a foreign land. This never-healing wound is the unfathomable depth of every person. All our ventures and exploits, all our acts and dreams, are bridges designed to overcome the separation and reunite us with the world and our fellow beings. Each person's life and the collective history of humanity can thus be seen as an attempt to reconstruct the original situation. An unfinished and endless cure for our divided condition.[2]

I understand the condition Paz describes. The pain of separation is called mourning, and if separation is permanent, the mourning can last a lifetime. When my husband of thirty-four years died, I felt the loneliness of separation. Friends tried to comfort me with words like, "You know where he is," to which I replied, "Yes, but I don't know where I am." Later a line from Iris Murdoch's *Jackson's Dilemma* struck me as being exactly right. A character who finds himself in deep mourning says, "I experienced an identity loss."

After Chick's death, I wrote in my diary: "Not only did I lose Chick, but I seem to have lost myself. I've gone missing! I mourn for my bright eyes, my lively gait, my flowing hair, my clear skin, my keen memory." I think mourning is a selfish act.

Eudora Welty defined this state as "love with the joy being drawn out of it" so that it becomes a painful ache.[3] Losing someone we love always causes a deep ache.

Now I must admit that I am both alone, as in "this is a wonderful opportunity to write," and lonely, which is a selfish mourning for loss.

I am alone, lonely—and single.

One night I went to bed the wife of the beloved ex-bishop and awoke the next day a "single adult." My first church calling after Chick's death was "singles representative." As I explained to the bishop, I didn't feel single, and I was tart with the social services clerk who called to ask when my marriage ended. "My marriage didn't end!" I replied indignantly. "My husband died!"

Previously my experience with "singleness" had been brief: I married in my late twenties, among the last in my set, aware that I was an incipient old maid or member of the "special interest" class. I graduated from college, earned an M.A., and taught at BYU before tying the knot. Our wedding list was bloated with former loves and their families. At the reception, we greeted them in shifts as the line wound around the block—a cherished memory.

As a married woman with children, I cultivated unmarried friends who were savvy in areas others were not and could discuss subjects other than the accomplishments of their children. During my husband's bishoping years in the late seventies, I enjoyed the eighty or so unmarried members in our ward. They were smart, talented people who left me lonely for them when they were gerrymandered into the new singles ward. I felt the depletion as I did when the Spanish members left for their new ward. The whole concept of segregated wards bothered me. Would the next move be a ward for parents of three children, I wondered.

When the bishop of the singles ward referred to himself as the "father of 400 children," I got a whiff of another problem. These hard-working adults are seen as immature because they are unmarried. I suppose it's true that marriage does mature a person, but then so does almost every other experience in life. Singles wards have a single purpose—not that singles wards haven't led to some pretty singular partnerships, including those of my two sons.

But what of those who do not succeed in finding a mate at church? Are they less worthy? Maybe this is why the authorities have decreed that those who are older than thirty-five and have not found a mate should be thrown back into their geographical congregations. The subject that rarely comes up in church circles is whether those people who are inherently solitary, even hermetic, might prefer to remain alone, and if so, is there a place for them in the kingdom?

Despite my doubts about my suitability as the ward singles representative, I accepted the calling with the caveat that I would excuse myself from dances and matchmaking socials. I had been warned by a friend who had chaired a large singles conference. Watching from the sidelines, she had noticed older, overweight men choose younger, slimmer dance partners. My friend, an attractive fifty-something, was herself considered unsuitable by sixty-something men who still hoped to father children.

When I explained my misgivings to him, the bishop told me my duties were to simply befriend single members and report their needs to him. After a few weeks, I reported that most of the singles were well integrated into the ward and were longtime members, mostly widowed. Some of the younger women had left the singles ward and moved into ours. I noticed that these members were seldom called on to pray in church and reported this to the stake singles committee, pointing out that we are all single since we will be saved for our individual faith. We all deserve to be treated as fully functioning members and to be given callings and assigned home teachers.

My career as the singles representative led me to accept the invitation to be the keynote speaker at a singles conference in a neighboring state. My talk, "An Eye Single," emphasized the advantages of life without a partner. I quoted research findings that showed single women in the church were more faithful and better educated than others. I used Juanita Brooks's analogy where she quoted her father's advice:

> I'm a cowboy, and I have learned that if I ride in the herd, I am lost—totally helpless. One who rides counter to it is trampled and killed. One who only trails behind means little, because he leaves all responsibility to others. It is the cowboy who rides the edge of the herd, who sings and calls and makes himself heard who helps direct the course. . . . So don't lose yourself, and don't ride away and desert the outfit. Ride the edge of the herd and be alert, but know your directions, and call out loud and clear. Chances are, you won't make any difference, but on the other hand, you just might.[4]

I compared the single, faithful member to the lone cowboy riding herd and helping direct the course of the church. Singles, I said, can be in the world but not of the world, able to report from a unique perspective. They can lend their talents by volunteering in neglected areas. I told of the contributions of unmarried people to the publication of *Dialogue,* those who would come to my basement and edit, proofread, do the accounting, and perform myriad other tasks. Their shared labor was rewarding to them. They pronounced our staff meetings a "safe" and enjoyable place to be. I appreciated these good people for their unselfish service, their wisdom, their experience, their sense of humor. I hoped to pass on this hope and faith to my audience as I pointed out that singles are fast becoming the majority in the church and should therefore exercise some influence and (benevolent) power.

But the discussion afterward revealed a prevailing sense of hopelessness. Many so longed for the companionship of marriage and children that my words barely penetrated. Conditioned by a culture that asks "In the heavens are parents single?" they could not be content with earthly bachelorhood or spinsterhood. The myth of the rugged individual, solitary hero that is so engrained in American culture, was not part of their dreams or visions.

And who can blame them? As one of my single friends put it, "I grieve for what I have never had." Each morning she awakens to the knowledge that she is not first in anyone's life except her own. The church places the married state at the pinnacle of achievement in this life and the life to come. Most members find it difficult to think that any other state could be as rewarding. Of course, we are chasing an ideal world in which all marriages are loving, unselfish, rewarding.

My own loneliness stems from the loss of what I did have, the companionship of a good man, someone to process the day with, someone to recall the good times and to plan for more. Someone to share life's sorrows—a buffer zone and backup for the talents I lacked. Someone to feel secure with. Someone to laugh at my foibles. Though presently alone and lonely, I realize I am one of the lucky ones.

Now I feel ashamed for thinking I could talk to genuine singles about the reality of their world. It's true that in the final analysis we are all single. We all came into the world alone and will all go out the same way. But it is also true that we all hope for loving arms at both ends of our lives, as well as in the middle.

If Gene England were still among us, I'm sure he could clarify for me the paradox of "the One within the Many." It's the double life described by Willa Cather:

> One realizes that even in harmonious families there is this double life: the group life, which is the one we can observe in our neighbor's household, and, underneath, another—secret and passionate and intense—which is the real life. . . . One realizes that human relationships are the tragic necessity of human life; that they can never be wholly satisfactory, that every ego is half the time greedily seeking them and half the time pulling away from them. In those simple relationships of loving husband and wife, affectionate sisters, children and grandmother, there are innumerable shades of sweetness and anguish which make up the pattern of our lives.[5]

Cather hints at the inherent worm in the rose. Even in the best of families, disappointment strikes.

We emphasize the individual, the One, the Lost Sheep, the uncreated intelligence, the Son who stepped forward in the spirit world and said "Here am I, send me," while recalling that we Mormons are also part of the most successful communitarian emigration in history. We are people who were led intact into the desert to create one of the most successful city-states in modern times. Our ancestors endured amazing hardships, partly because everyone in the community felt called of God to a unique purpose and meaning. Not that they were exempt from loneliness and mourning, but they had group support to steady them.

Perhaps the ideal situation would be to place each individual within a community of caring souls who look out for one another, no matter what one's status. In other words, a community of saints in these latter days—the ideal ward. But given the tension between the church's continuing emphasis on two halves making a whole in marriage and the growing number of singles, it is likely that for most singles this will remain an ideal.

I am trying to be less self-pitying. I think of a quotation from a quirky little novel where the narrator, a single woman in her forties, comes to terms with her lot. "I try no longer to think of my singleness," she says, "as something that has happened to me; something like a car accident, something unfortunate and unfair, something that I have suffered through no fault of my own. . . . I am not always successful in this endeavour, . . . but I can think of my singleness as something I have chosen." She adds that although she doesn't know why or how she chose it, she feels good about taking responsibility for her state, for her own life. "It is not asceticism or abnegation or martyrdom. It is not a punishment, a condemnation, an abomination, an embarrassment, an inversion of the natural order, or a cruel joke played upon me by God."[6] She decides that simply having a relationship with a man is not the answer, nor is any relationship or any one event.

Like married people, singles can choose to live authentic, fulfilling, adventurous lives even though it may be more challenging for them to do so. As for me, I intend to sit here in my condo and accept the fact that I chose to be here. I could have made other choices, but I fully choose to live alone in this place and at this time. Even if I am not to blame for everything that has brought me here, I can still accept responsibility for it. Another paradox!

My research into the life of Lowell L. Bennion reminds me of his important sayings about "the purpose of life [being] self-realization and fulfillment for all people, . . . to achieve quality living, to enlarge our souls, to live and be what God made us. . . . The purpose of life is within life, not outside it."[7] That goes for all of us, whether single or not.

My philosophical friend sends me this advice, and I think I will abide by it: "Maybe the thing is not to meditate on 'the meaning of living alone,' but just to do it and thereby come to understand what it is to live alone. It is simply Living Alone, not good, not bad, but different from living with someone. And one has to learn this new self or rather hitherto unknown aspect-of-self. For me, [too much] pondering led to paralysis/inertia. What about just watching this [new] Mary and make friends with her and discover all that she needs and all that she needs to discard?"[8]

So, rather than lose my identity, I am going about finding and developing another side of it. I suppose that's what Christ meant when he promised that if we lose ourselves in service to Him, we will find ourselves. As Stephen Mitchell says, the gospel according to Jesus is "simply this: that the love we all long for in our innermost heart is already present, beyond longing. . . . Entering the kingdom of God means feeling, as if we were floating in the womb of the universe, that we are being taken care of, always, at every moment."[9] In my loneliest single moments, I feel taken care of.

[2004]

## Notes

1. "Bereft," in *The Poetry of Robert Frost* (New York: Modern Library, Random House, 1946), 275.

2. Octavio Paz, *In Search of the Present: Nobel Lecture, 1990* (Cambridge: Harvard University Press, 1990), 10–11.

3. Eudora Welty, *The Bride of Innisfallen and Other Stories* (New York: Harcourt Brace, 1977), 81.

4. Davis Bitton and Maureen Beecher, "'Riding Herd': A Conversation with Juanita Brooks," *Dialogue: A Journal of Mormon Thought* 9 (Spring 1974), 23.

5. Nancy Mitford, *Savage Beauty: The Life of Edna St. Vincent Millay* (New York: Random House, 2001), frontispiece.

6. Diane Schoemperlen, *Our Lady of the Lost and Found* (New York: Penguin Books, 2002), 321–22.

7. Mary L. Bradford, *Lowell L. Bennion: Teacher, Counselor, Humanitarian* (Salt Lake City: Dialogue Foundation, 1994), 112.

8. Lili LeCain to Mary Bradford, October 4, 2003.

9. Stephen Mitchell, *The Gospel According to Jesus: A New Translation and Guide to His Essential Teachings for Believers and Unbelievers* (New York: HarperCollins, 1991), 10, 12.

# IT TAKES MANY VILLAGES

Whenever I'm asked why I'm a Mormon, my first thought is, "Where else would I go?" The church is my village and my home.

I attended another church while staying in Eyeries, a village in southwest Ireland, for several months over a three-year period. The Catholic congregation welcomed me, even inviting me to sing in the choir. One of the bachelor farmers complimented me on my no-drinking-or-smoking clean living, adding that he himself had "never touched the drink." He recited the pledge he took as a twelve-year-old. I replied that I, too, had taken a pledge called the Word of Wisdom. I recited a few lines for him. I enjoyed going to church there, especially since meetings were only about forty-five minutes long.

In my mind the priest was an Irish version of the late Lowell Bennion, whom I so admired all my life. Lowell was the LDS Institute director at the University of Utah and humanitarian whose emphasis was on service to the needy. The Irish priest had trained young men and boys to build homes for the elderly at a previous parish. He gave me a blessing by crossing himself, then laying his hands on my head: "I bless you that you will always have the spirit of Christ in your life."

These experiences did not convert me to Catholicism. Like historian D. Michael Quinn, I am a DNA Mormon. The church belongs to me and I to it. I don't intend to leave. Sometimes I feel that the church is leaving me, but I intend to stick around anyway. I am comforted by the thought that the church structure we know is a temporal plan. For now, I need some structure in my life. I may not need so many strictures, but I need the association with people in the church. In the journey that is my life, the most amazing friends and family have been nearby to succor me, accompany me, advise and nourish me. Although I have friends from outside the church, my really deep bonds have come through Church connections.

## Childhood

I was imprinted with LDS convictions as a child when I ran freely over my dad's little acre in East Mill Creek, outside of Salt Lake City. It was our food chain during the Great Depression. We never felt deprived. We ate fresh fruits and vegetables from our garden and meat from the calves or pigs Dad killed once a year. We drank milk from our own cows, Daisy and Buttercup. From my mother, Lavinia Mitchell Lythgoe, I inherited a love for the printed word and the arts. From my father, Leo Lythgoe, I inherited a love for good hard work and the great outdoors. From them both, I came to love the gospel of Jesus Christ. Neither of my parents was educated past the tenth grade, but they supported their children as we chose to pursue higher education.

Through school classes and church dances, I found I loved books and stories. While others played kickball during grade-school recess, I gathered a little circle of fans and read them my stories. In my early years, I sensed that the parables of Jesus and the stories in the Bible were more convincing than sermons. (The fact that I have not fulfilled my childhood and teenage dream of becoming a fiction writer is partly due to the fact that it was educated out of me and partly because the stories published by writers like Virginia Sorensen were more exciting than anything I could dream up.) The diary I kept from ages thirteen to twenty-two shows that those years were filled with delightful experiences, encouraging teachers, loyal friends, and church leaders who seemed devoted to my development. In the ward, I learned to give a speech, teach a lesson, write and act in plays and skits, and tend to children. My two younger brothers, Tom and Dennis, and my late-arriving sister, Gaye, were my constant companions.

## University

The University of Utah was another kind of village where I signed up for classes at the Institute of Religion under Lowell Bennion, George Boyd, and T. Edgar Lyon. These dovetailed with my classes across the street at the university. I remember thinking, "I am living a charmed life. I want to write about it some day."

As I reflect on those years, I echo Laurel Thatcher Ulrich's words at a commencement speech in which she said her life was anchored by Dr. William Mulder at the university and by Dr. Lowell Bennion across the street at the institute. Hats off to them and the other fine professors who helped me earn an M.A. in English and gave me the skills for a lifetime of learning. My great teachers used the Socratic method and asked meaningful questions, which I found more important than memorizing answers. Brother Bennion once wrote on the board: "What is your philosophy of life?" We shallow students had no idea what that might mean. We parroted clichés we had heard in church while he showed us how superficial our answers were.

Brother Bennion criticized the approach sometimes taken by teachers who seem to ask, "What am I thinking?" instead of "What are YOU thinking?" Life is not a giant *Jeopardy!* game where we are expected to read the minds of our leaders and parrot a response. I believe that the ability to ask questions from deep within the soul leads us to understanding and faith.

## Great Adventures

My first full-time job took me to Brigham Young University, where I taught English with another group of creative thinkers—Bruce Clark, Marden Clark, Clinton Larsen, Jeannette Morell, Leonard Rice, and Orea Tanner, to name a few. I was happy and stimulated in my work but unhappy in church. In my ward I was a "Special-Interest" or unmarried member with the calling of assistant roll-taker in one of my ward's several Gospel Doctrine classes. I took to traveling to Salt Lake City nearly every Sunday, so friends and family there thought I was attending church in Provo while the Provoans believed I was in church in Salt Lake. I was going inactive and nobody realized it—not even I.

Luckily, I began to date someone I had known at the University of Utah who was then teaching economics at BYU while finishing his Ph.D. from Harvard: Charles Henry Bradford, or "Chick," as everyone called him. We had similar backgrounds, the same basic worldview. We held slightly different political views—he a Republican, I a Democrat—but this was before today's polarization into blues and reds. We blended well. We were purple. Power to the Purple!

After our marriage in 1957, I was immediately called as Gospel Doctrine teacher. A few weeks later we accepted with alacrity the opportunity for Chick to work for Senator Wallace Bennett in the U.S. Congress. What a great adventure! Marriage saved me from inactivity and plunged me into the vortex of child-rearing and ward and stake activities. The Arlington Virginia Ward became my next village. The ward had an impressive history. Its founders built the chapel with their own hands. We thus joined a group of young couples who reared our children together and, because our parents were not nearby, became our own family.

The ward was a healthy mixture of students and government professionals who were readers and thinkers, determined to benefit from the advantages of living near the nation's capital. The Mormons were strong in the church, and we decided we liked the region despite dire warnings from our Utah family and friends who spoke of the impossibility of rearing Mormon children "in the East." Some expected us to return home to Zion as soon as we could, but we believed we were already in our own Zion.

## Dialogue

When Eugene England and friends founded *Dialogue: A Journal of Mormon Thought* in 1966, I volunteered. I saw my support for the journal as part of being "anxiously engaged in a good cause and do[ing] many things of [my] own free will" (D&C 58:27)—a principle I had been taught in my youth. The Church's in-house organs couldn't print all the fine work we young people wanted to write. My involvement put me back in touch with former school friends and colleagues. It was a yeasty time when all kinds of issues were waiting to be questioned.

Gene started me out on my career as a personal essayist when he asked me to write a regular section in the journal. I had no idea that ten years later I would become *Dialogue*'s first female editor at exactly the time when the women's movement was heating up in this country. I have to thank Bob Rees for "calling" me to be the editor. He remains a friend and brother. I was already in my forties when I became the editor but was still wonderfully naïve. Imagine my surprise upon learning that, speaking from deep within my cozy cocoon, I was now an "alternative voice" in the church. When I went to Salt Lake City to keep an appointment with the Church Historian, he refused to see me. "I refuse to talk to the editor of *Dialogue*," he said. I was also refused as a speaker at the BYU women's conference by Dallin Oaks, who said: "We can't have just anybody speaking here." I was acquainted with Elder Oaks and knew he had written for *Dialogue*, so his response surprised me. After I had published an article in the *Ensign* on Mormons in Washington, D.C., an editor there said if he had known I was to become *Dialogue*'s editor, he would not have published my article. Whenever I think of this response, I smile, knowing that my article now resides in the cornerstone of the Washington Temple. I am amazed at policies like these. We are all church members. Why can't leaders sit down and discuss the issues that threaten to divide us?

During my years as editor (1976–1982), I worked with a well-grounded board of editors and a staff for whom no task was too small or too large. While I was still with *Dialogue*, blacks received the priesthood, the church became more international, women spoke out about their rights and responsibilities, and important parts of Mormon intellectual history came to light. Although the so-called Camelot under Leonard Arrington closed down, professional history writing continued. Lester Bush, associate editor during my tenure, followed his ground-breaking article on blacks in the church with significant studies of birth control and other subjects. We celebrated the church's sesquicentennial and published the first papers delivered at conferences of the Mormon History Association and Association for Mormon Letters. We cooperated with other independent publications such as *Sunstone* and *Exponent II*, exchanging articles and advice.

This was exciting work, which I somehow did while my bishop-husband ran the ward and my children grew up. Professionally, I consulted with government agencies on their writing and led workshops on editing and speaking, a position that came to me through my Mormon network. When it was time to move the journal to Utah under Jack and Linda Newell, we knew it was strong enough to survive. Its fortieth anniversary was celebrated in 2006.

After my *Dialogue* sojourn, I was entrusted with the life of my mentor and teacher, Lowell Bennion, whose biography I wrote. Thanks to *Dialogue* and the editing advice of wonderful friends such as Gene

England, Lavina Fielding Anderson, and Emma Lou Thayne, I was able to publish the story of his life just before he died in 1995.

## Family and Friends

A reporter once asked Esther Peterson, that great and famous activist from Utah, what advice she would give young women wanting a career in public service. She answered, somewhat surprisingly, "Marry the right man." Chick's unfailing support of everything I tried to do was my strongest pillar of faith. When he passed away in 1991, my ward village, along with my friends in Utah and elsewhere, mourned with me, comforting me during the stages of grief. My three children, Steve, Lorraine, and Scott, along with their twelve children, have among them some of Chick's qualities, and, when I am with them, I don't miss him as much.

My mourning took me to Ireland, that green, grieving land, accompanied by strong women friends. One of these, Sue Booth Paxman, former editor of *Exponent II,* decided to settle in Ireland. As Sue Booth-Forbes, she opened a writers' and artists' retreat in a little paradise in southwest Cork. She and the people I met there created a village much like my childhood one, which was the perfect spot for me to write and heal. Sue is one of the many friends who have stayed with me through darkness and light. They have given me advice and shelter through long nights of grief and laughed me out of depression. They have helped me rear my children and publish my work. Besides the women I have mentioned, a long line of men, including the mentors and colleagues I have already named, has opened doors for me to both friendship and understanding. It gives lie to the belief that a man and woman cannot be true friends. They can!

Now I am living in my last village. Seven years ago I sold my house in Arlington and moved twenty miles away into a gated retirement community near my daughter. What I thought would be a peaceful old age devoted to writing my memoirs has proven just as challenging as my other sojourns, partly because I am suddenly a widow in a church of young married people. Shades of Special Interest! If ever I would leave the church, it would be out of sheer boredom. One source of frustration at church comes from the deadening influence of assigning subjects to speakers—usually the same subject each week to all the speakers. Though some are experienced enough to turn any topic into a stimulating sermon, most simply resort to a computer index of suitable quotations, thereby losing the personal touch. Lowell Bennion's way of organizing—choosing a topic dear to your heart, then supporting it with scriptures, experience, and prayer—is lost. I used to look forward to the quirky, humorous, personal experiences we heard in people's homilies.

In spite of this, I remain grateful to the structure of the Church, through which I have experienced spiritual blessings, beginning with a healing blessing administered to me at the age of three weeks. Just home from the hospital, I had contracted pneumonia and was turning blue. The doctor had given up on me. My mother recorded in her diary that Bishop Howick stopped in and performed a healing miracle—I was a miracle baby. Since then I have received many priesthood blessings that, if they did not heal me, gave me the courage to carry on. When I was a freshman at the University of Utah, my mother contracted pneumonia. My grandmother ordered me to "take your brothers and pray for your mother." It seemed that my mother's fate depended on it—and she was healed.

Chick suffered from a form of muscular dystrophy. Years into our marriage, he confided that many young women he had dated had expressed fear about bearing children with this hereditary disease. He had taken this to Harold B. Lee, a former school principal and family friend who had become an apostle. Elder Lee gave Chick a blessing and advised him to "be patient" because he would yet meet "a girl with enough faith."

When I became pregnant with our firstborn, Stephen, Chick arranged a meeting with Apostle Lee, who blessed me that my baby would be free of the disease. When sixteen years later Stephen was diagnosed with muscular dystrophy, I had a strange reaction. I recalled that one of Brother Bennion's favorite scriptures was this from Micah: "What does the Lord require of thee, but to do justly, and to love mercy, and to walk humbly with thy God?" (Micah 6:8) From this scripture, I came to understand that justice and mercy were primary qualities and that we should be humble in recognizing that God would walk with us—not ahead or behind us. In meeting the news of Stephen's affliction this way, I became internally satisfied that God would not or could not intervene in the progress of this inherited disease that had already struck generations of worthy Bradfords. That left me with the fact that our child would have to suffer. I took Steve to see a specialist, a doctor who seemed to know of every case in America. She told him: "Look at your father. He is your example of what you can accomplish."

At the time Stephen was meeting with her, I was sitting in the waiting room in deep despair. I thought, "If only I could take this disease on myself." Then Stephen walked smiling into the room. "Mom, there is something I can do," he exclaimed. On our way home, he added, "I believe I chose you and dad in the preexistence, and I would do it again!" At that moment I knew that even if God had not eradicated the disease, he had given us a great blessing in a son as courageous as his father. Chick was able to turn a disability into an ability—the ability to understand and inspire others.

That the combined prayers of a ward, a stake, and family members could not stop death from taking my husband leaves me in awe at the mysteries of the universe. As I face the end of my life on this earth without my partner, I lean on the gospel of Jesus Christ as I see it joyously lived around me.

[2011]

# SWEET HOME:
# AN EPILOGUE

I am always leaving home. And yet, in a way, I have never left home. My mother used to say, in mingled irritation and amusement, that I was a "gadder." I would go out to play as soon as I awoke. I would cry if she pronounced me too ill to go to school. Later, I would feign health so that she couldn't keep me out of school. In his later years, Dad marveled whenever I came to town. "She doesn't even have a car and yet she gets all over this bloomin' country!"

My eagerness to leave home, of course, was buttressed by the assurance that I could always come home. Dad would come for me almost anywhere, first in his '28 Chevy, and then in his truck. Toward the end of her life, Mother asked me not to stay with her anymore because my constant comings and goings made her nervous. I tried to explain that my interest in the world outside of home derived from the security and love I had there. But I think I understand her concern now that I have grown children who come and go.

After our marriage, Chick and I moved to Arlington, Virginia, and it took eight years before we finally bought a house and gave up thoughts of returning to Utah. One night, as we crossed Key Bridge into Arlington, I gazed across the Potomac at the now-familiar spires of Georgetown University and finally uttered the words, "This is home." Why did it take me so long?

The cliché—they can take the girl out of Utah, but they can't take Utah out of the girl—still holds. Even when we do go away to build our own families and homes, we must come to terms with the homes and the people who shaped the experience of home for us.

My parents lived in the same home for fifty-five years. As far as I know, they had no desire to leave it. Because I lived there until my marriage, I mourned the selling of the house almost as much as the deaths of my parents. The house was a symbol of permanence. Yet my generation was willing to move away, and our children have already lived in several apartments and two houses. Still we have the collective homes of our parents and grandparents and all the others who have taken us in.

Mormons tend to shape their sense of a homelife on their theology of an afterlife. In my youth, Lorenzo Snow's couplet was widely quoted: "As man now is, God once was; as God now is, man may become." As a child it gave me confidence, and I looked forward not only to the creation of worlds but to the creation of stories and poems that would spring to life through my perfected imagination.

Today, we don't hear the godhood theme as much. We hear more about living righteously enough to return to our heavenly home. This is expressed in the popular children's song, "I Am a Child of God," which has almost reached the status of scripture. In Richard Cracroft and Neal Lambert's Mormon literature volume, *A Believing People,* it was printed in the contemporary poetry section and was called, appropriately enough, "Home Literature." The last verse says: "Lead me, guide me, walk beside me; / Help me find the way. / Teach me all that I must do / To live with him some day." The song, "O My Father," by Eliza R. Snow, Lorenzo's sister, had said it before: "When I leave this frail existence / When I lay this mortal by/ Father, Mother, may I meet you / In your royal courts on high? / Then, at length, when I've completed / All you sent me forth to do, / With your mutual approbation / Let me come and dwell with you."

After growing up with the admonition of President Snow to become independent, virtuous souls capable of greatness, and the idea of teaching children to walk away from us, I was hearing that perhaps it would be better to concentrate on the values of home. I now realize how little I understand this earth and whatever other earths there are in the universe, and I sympathize with those who are more comfortable with that simple verse inviting us back home than with intimations of godhood.

I have been leaving and returning to my home in symbolic ways all of my life. I believe that, as we carry the spark of divinity within us from our eternal home, we also carry our earthly homes inside us. They

tug at us with the warm feelings we had there; they push us out with
the security and confidence we learned there; they pull us back with the
love and history of generations.

[1990]

# "THEY ALSO SERVE"
# (WHO ONLY SIT AND WRITE)

The Mormon religion is an undeniable part of my being. A descendant of Utah pioneers, I was the first child of parents who never questioned the faith but merely accepted its precepts as facts of life. One of these is the right of every member to certain blessings, among them healing and health. My parents believed that I was actually an incarnation of that blessing, a kind of "miracle baby." At three weeks, I contracted pneumonia. According to the family legend, the doctor had given up, and I was turning blue when the bishop of our ward (congregation), known throughout the neighborhood for the "gift of healing," appeared at our door. He and my father anointed my head with oil, placed their hands upon my head, said a prayer, and restored me to life.

Growing up as a miracle baby was both an advantage and a burden. The miraculous healing meant great expectations for me. I believed that I had been spared for a purpose, and as I grew older, I connected this purpose with writing and publishing. I have a memory of myself at age seven or so in my "Let's Pretend" mood. I am holding one of the stories I was forever writing and reading to anyone who would listen. I have shaped it into a scroll, tied a ribbon around it, and am pretending to hand it over to a New York publisher. The publisher accepts with alacrity, of course.

As an adolescent, and after I learned a bit more about the process of writing, I formed an ambition to write "for the church." This meant volunteering for any writing job that presented itself, from the ward newsletter to the ward play. Though I was disappointed that the articles and poetry I sent to church magazines and newspapers were not always accepted, I was actually proud of my rejection slips, because they made me feel professional. My output was welcomed by local church members, however, and as I grew older, I was able to place more of my poems and articles.

Because of constant encouragement by teachers, family, and friends, I entered the University of Utah in the early Fifties with high hopes. This state university, in fact, offered a group of dedicated, mostly male, mentors and teachers who seemed determined to help. With the women's movement just a smudge on the horizon, the university and the Mormon Church's Institute of Religion across the street gave both girls and boys every chance to excel. Or so it seemed to me. Dr. Lowell L. Bennion, sociologist, philosopher, and religionist, ran the Institute, which included classes taught by him and two other gifted teachers on everything from world religions to courtship and marriage. I took all of the classes, graduating from the Institute after I had finished my assigned project: the revision and editing of two of Bennion's books. These books were very popular throughout the church, especially with young people seeking to combine their religion with their secular studies. This was my first creative editing experience.

Lowell Bennion, whom we lovingly called "Brother B.," became the very model of my religion, the one who clearly practiced what he preached, a humane, Christian version of the Mormon faith—development through service and study. Through his "work parties" and various service projects in the larger community, we students were taught to seek out the less fortunate and to forget our own troubles. At the same time, he was always available to listen to our troubles. He challenged us through reading, discussion, lecture, and prayer. Even now the still small voice of my conscience often speaks in his voice. He was both nurturing and challenging, in the same way my father was. I never thought to call these traits male or female: They were simply human with a touch of the divine.

I spent seven years at the University, emerging with an M.A. in English and three years experience as a teacher of freshman English. I cherish my rosy memories of that time when "boys and girls together" studied in a kind of charmed, preactivist glow.

Because writing was never really portrayed as a viable goal, I chose to become an English teacher. In spite of the many opportunities given me to write and to edit, only teaching, nursing, and stenography seemed possible for a girl. Since professors of English were usually required to write, I decided that the academic track was the one for me. I departed therefore for the "Lord's University," Brigham Young at Provo, Utah, and my first full-time job as instructor of English.

It was rewarding to be paid for a task I found so enjoyable that I would gladly have volunteered for it. Freshman Mormon students were easy to teach because of the cultural icons we shared. And the salary, which seemed exorbitant at the time, would support me in my plans for a Ph.D., preferably at Stanford, sometime in the future.

But as my religion had taught me to reverence intelligence, placing it next to godliness in the scriptures, it had also taught me to look for a suitable mate. In my early twenties, I had aspired to serve a foreign mission for the Church but had been refused on the grounds that I was young and attractive enough to be married instead. This was my introduction to sexism in the church.

It so happened that Charles Bradford, a young economics instructor and friend from the University of Utah, was a suitable choice. After a brief courtship, we planned a late summer wedding.

It was then that I was summoned to the office of my department head for questioning. Why hadn't I informed him of my marriage *before* signing my contract for the next year? When I looked puzzled, he informed me that university policy required married women instructors to switch to halftime or to give up teaching entirely. Since I had already signed, he would content himself with consigning me to an office full of graduate students. If I couldn't give up my contract, I could at least give up my privacy!

That was the second consciousness-raising "click" in my sheltered life. Perhaps this made it easier to follow my husband to Washington, D.C., where he could both work for a senator and finish his own Ph.D. I have often wondered why I was so quick to give up my own plans. I can't really blame my gentle and open-minded husband. I am sure he would have supported me if I had applied at one of the many universities in the area instead of getting on as clerk-typist at the Library of Congress. It was part of the culture of the time. A Master's degree for a woman was rare in my circles, and, though I was praised for it, most people expected me to settle down with children and live happily ever after. So I accepted a stop-gap position while waiting for our first child. (It is amusing to recall that my supervisor, who recognized my M.A. by giving me research assignments in the main reading room, was very understanding when I kept skipping work with morning sickness. Instead of giving me the sack, he advised me to "keep the tummy full.")

I entered wifehood and motherhood in the bosom of newfound friends in Washington and in our ward in Arlington, Virginia, where I was asked to teach literature to the women's auxiliary of the church— the Relief Society. Soon thereafter I experienced my third feminist "click." The choir leader in the ward, charged with the Christmas cantata for Sunday services, asked me to give a short sermon as part of the program. After which she informed me of the bishop's instructions: I was not to discuss "doctrine." If women were to be allowed to speak from the pulpit at all, it had to be on safe, "literary" subjects.

This was my first hint that a married woman might be a threat in the pulpit. Mormonism is a lay church, so most members can expect to be asked to speak. Since public speaking was one of my hobbies, I was always willing. I recall myself at fifteen lambasting the ward for what I perceived as unchristian backbiting and gossip among the members. At another time I emotionally expressed my thanks to God for the miracle of my mother's recovery from pneumonia. Public thanks were expected. As a young girl and later as a young woman, I was often grateful for the many mercies in my life.

Under the influence of Brother B., I had learned that all should serve according to their talents. I had been given ample opportunity in college to show off as a speaker, a teacher, and as a presider over meetings. My attitude toward the male "priesthood holders" therefore could be best summed up in the line from one of the hymns, "as the dew from heaven distilling": The priesthood helps all to develop their talents. The men may bring priesthood power into the room, but men and women share equally in its blessings. Priesthood, therefore, had been presented to me not so much as a political force as a call to serve. My father, a gentle, hardworking man, had used the priesthood to restore the family to health, to pray with us, and to cry with us in our travail. He had served as a missionary, but according to him he had never spoken or prayed in public. My mother, too, was backward about public display. They both had lived their religion more quietly than did any of their four children. I was already married before I fully realized that some Mormons were interpreting the priesthood as male privilege to which no woman, no matter how spiritual, could aspire. But Mormon scripture gives this advice to the church: "No power or influence can or ought to be maintained by virtue of the priesthood, only by persuasion, by long-suffering, by gentleness and meekness, and by love unfeigned; by kindness, and pure knowledge, which shall greatly enlarge the soul without hypocrisy, and without guile" (D&C 121:31–42). Any other behavior meant "amen to the priesthood of that man"! Meaning *finis*! Brother B. had never been interested in the trappings of power. He describes it this way: "I don't have any interest in being exalted. I'd like to be in the presence of Christ, be a co-worker, but I believe that he who would save his life shall lose it, and he that would lose his life shall find it."[1]

Well, I survived the "literary speech" and lived to give doctrinal speeches. For the next ten years I stayed home, more or less, teaching church classes and tutoring Mormon students. When our third and last child was safely in school, I fell into an illness that my doctor diagnosed with these words: "Mrs. Bradford, when will you get back to your teaching? There is no illness like that of unused talent."

As if on cue, a member of the ward who happened to be a top executive in a government agency appeared with an offer of a job-consulting and teaching in his office. This miraculously coincided with the founding of an independent journal, the first of its kind: *Dialogue: A Journal of Mormon Thought*. The editors, graduate students at Stanford and former disciples of Brother B. and the Institute program, asked me to join their editorial board. Voila! The job and the journal lifted my depression.

In the first issue the editors announced that "a new generation of Mormons has arisen" who are "curious and welltrained and committed to church activity" and who wish to bring "their faith into dialogue with human experience as a whole and to foster artistic and scholarly achievement based on their cultural heritage."[2]

I was one of these young Mormons. I wanted to be part of the plan for improving the writing of the church. Much in-house writing was disappointing. I felt the need for challenging fiction and poetry and for meaty historical and doctrinal studies. I had no idea then that ten years later I would become the journal's first woman editor when women's issues were paramount, during the excommunication of Sonia Johnson. When Robert Rees, who succeeded England and Johnson, passed the torch to me, he emphasized that "it was time for a woman" to take over, but with one piece of advice: "Remember that your title is 'editor,' not 'mother.'" He sensed that I would have difficulty separating roles, with everything being sandwiched between family responsibilities.

*Dialogue* did become a kind of cottage industry because of its office in the commodious basement of our home in Arlington, Virginia, where talented volunteers, including my own children, gathered to edit, write, type, and talk. I fed them with one hand, managed them with the other. The result was almost seven years of high-quality publishing in a remarkable degree of harmony. Now when I gaze at the shelf we produced, twenty-one issues in all, I feel that I did fulfill my childhood ambition, to write and publish for the people who mean the most to me—Mormons.

Another of my favorite scriptures admonishes us to be "anxiously engaged in a good cause" and to "bring to pass much righteousness of our own free will" (D&C 58:27). I came to believe that my contributions were to keep the journal alive during difficult economic times and to publish on women's themes.

I had begun to study women's history, especially Mormon pioneer history, in the early seventies. In 1973 I had assisted in the editing of *Dialogue*'s first women's issue. Edited by a group of Boston Mormon women, it led to the founding of *Exponent II*, a newspaper for Mormon women, now ten years old. This group also published *Mormon Sisters*, a landmark volume of historical essays that they dedicated to Leonard Arrington, the first church historian to open the archives freely to women scholars. These women and other trained women historians began excavating the accomplishments of those pioneer women who at great risk settled in Utah and educated themselves as teachers, writers, suffragists, and artists while rearing large, sometimes polygamous families. The consciousness-raising "click" I experienced through this period was uplifting and motivating.

A few of these descendants of Mormon pioneers formed an organization called Mormons for ERA (MERA) as a protest against the church's anti-ERA campaign. They expected me to join them, hinting that *Dialogue* should officially support their cause. I felt that personal activism on my part was inappropriate, since as editor I was representing not myself alone but the subscribers and the board of editors as well. Looking back, I see that I would not have joined anyway. I am not a joiner, a sign-carrier, nor a protestor at heart.

In 1978 *Dialogue* was preparing a "tutorial" on the ERA by a woman lawyer who favored it but was laying out arguments pro and con in a reasonable way.

The year before that, I had been asked to become a "spokesperson" by one of the bishops in the area. I had replied that I was not interested in becoming a spokesperson, either for or against. "I just want to get my magazine out," I told him. I went on to say that I believed the very respectable history of the accomplishments of Mormon pioneer women combined with the present accomplishments of Mormon women should speak for themselves. Women, I said, can be trusted to think for themselves and to make up their own minds.

From then on, I was increasingly buttonholed at parties and meetings by angry, worried, or curious women and men who wanted to discuss the ERA. When the Relief Society was organized by the church to protest the ERA in Richmond, I told my diary: "Think what could be done if the women of the church could be mobilized so quickly for seven weeks of really important work!"

I still had little idea of the hysteria that could be generated by this issue, hysteria that would lead to Sonia's excommunication with its attendant media coverage. I resented being told that I should fight against it for no stronger reason that it would "not ennoble women." (This from the letter sent out from the First Presidency.) Nobility is a judgment reserved for posterity. On the other hand, I was less than enthusiastic about banner-tows over the temple grounds. Some things are sacred!

The atmosphere grew increasingly charged. Writers and reporters began calling me for quotations and background information. One of my statements was garbled enough in a local article that my stake president asked me to clarify. A television network wanted to interview me about my relationship with Sonia, an acquaintance of some years. When I offered to be interviewed about *Dialogue* instead, they lost interest. A short *Dialogue* interview aired in Salt Lake City sparked rumors that I had finally been recruited by ERA forces. Arguments heightened. Anti-ERA petitions appeared in Mormon chapels. My husband, who was then bishop of our ward, refused them, but the ward that shared our building did not. Seeing the petition on Sunday morning, my teenage daughter scandalized people by scrawling across it "This is sacrilegious!" Rumors and rumors of rumors were rife.

Sonia Johnson had seemed at first not much different from most Relief Society women I had known—outspoken, sincere, modest in many ways, yet eloquent and fiery when crossed. Bishop Willis, portrayed in the press as a tough FBI agent, was also a friend whose parents hailed from Dad's hometown. I felt sorry for them both. I could see how things had escalated until they were both trapped. I interviewed them both and researched the issues, trying to pick my way through the sticky labyrinth. Rumors reached *Dialogue* that if we dared publish anything the least bit sympathetic to Sonia, our own membership would be up for grabs. I polled our board, met with the staff and decided to publish an honest appraisal of Sonia and the events leading up to her excommunication. I decided to run an interview with Sonia with an introductory article about her life. The issue included a well-researched piece on the excommunication process and another on the church's diminished public image. After it came out, mail was evenly divided between letters calling us to repentance for publishing such a sympathetic work on an apostate and others complimenting us for our balance. We lost some subscriptions and picked up others. It was rumored that Sonia was unhappy with it, but several members of MERA renewed their subscriptions. We heard from no church authorities.

Though I still felt buffeted, I grew increasingly certain that I could make my best contributions to womankind by publishing the best of Mormon women writers and articles about them. It was clear that I could be both a seeker of truth and a reflector of the times in which I live. I wanted to chronicle these times and my own evolution. I found myself in a still center of a whirlwind where I felt a kind of peace as part of a network of reasonable, kindly people who were researching and publishing the best of Mormonism.

I and my *Dialogue* staff went on to design another women's issue: the 1982 anniversary issue. It celebrated the kaleidoscopic accomplishments of Mormon women on many artistic and academic levels. Contributions included articles and essays on women and the priesthood, the ERA, divorce, abortion, death. Its writers were scholars, poets, fiction writers, artists, dancers, and photographers. After interviewing 100 Mormon women for her photographic essay "In Context," Robin Hammond reported "beneath our Mormon facades, we differ and agree in a multitude of ways."

At the same time, *Dialogue* sponsored a personal essay contest, the brainchild of Marion Mangum of Olympus Publishing in Utah, who also wanted to make a contribution to the discussion. The result was a book, *Mormon Women Speak,* edited by me and published by her. These were honest pieces by a variety of both professional and amateur writers dealing with some of the most pressing issues in their lives. It was well received by a wide spectrum of women and men resulting in a second printing.

"Each of us carries a drive toward wholeness each of us struggles with outer and inner reconciliations. Each is in the process of becoming truly human." This line from one of the essays, "An Underground Journey toward Repentance" by Helen Stark, sums up my own feelings.

About this time, I accepted an invitation to speak on a panel at a meeting of the American Psychological Association on how religious women use their faith to cope with conflicts. I was given ten minutes to talk about how "committed Mormon women cope." When the *Journal of Pastoral Counseling* published the proceedings, I expanded mine into a brief article addressing the "articulate and outstanding" Mormon woman who elects to remain in the church. I pointed out that Mormon women find the strength to cope with increasing conflicts, both in and out of the church through emphasis on some indigenous Mormon traits: belief in the values of education and skill training, belief in the importance of family, and a natural penchant for networking. These mechanisms develop confidence to work for needed change in the church and in the larger society. I urged greater understanding of Mormon women as individuals with differing problems that belie the popular stereotype of sheep-like, obedient housewives waiting for their marching orders.

While preparing this article, I realized that I have become an activist almost by default. I have learned to clarify my positions gradually, not by flagrant protest but by quiet resolve. I have elected to remain in the church of my childhood and to work for change within it. Through my travels, in which I have talked with women around the church, and through my publishing ventures, I have developed a faith in the Church's ability to change. Organizational change is slow, to be sure, and I don't expect to see women given the priesthood in my lifetime. But then I hadn't expected to see it given to Blacks either, although I believed it had to happen sometime. Reforms could be made now by calling couples to church jobs currently held by men alone, by placing women on all governing boards of the church and by excising sexism from the lesson manuals and the rituals of the church.

When I feel especially discouraged, I remember that the three "clicks" that raised my consciousness twenty-five years ago have been silenced. BYU no longer requires women to give up their contracts for marriage; women are encouraged to serve missions, indeed, my daughter is serving in the Philippines; and women routinely speak on doctrinal issues every Sunday throughout the church. They don't speak about the ERA, of course, and I understand why many are impatient about that. I respect their impatience. I think the barnstorming does much to make it safe for brainstorming. There are shades and grades of activism, and there is a place for those who only sit and write. I hope to keep writing the truth as I see it. I am encouraged by the fact that my church raised millions of dollars for Ethiopian relief. I hope it will pay attention to the increasing fragility of this beautiful planet which Mormon doctrine says will one day be glorified in heaven as the Celestial Kingdom.

I admit that because my early role models were nurturing men, I find it impossible to believe that all men are to be mistrusted and that all male leaders—the patriarchy—should be stripped of authority. I do believe that it will be better for all when they learn to share that authority. I am still willing to work with the many men who have helped me grow and with the increasingly large number of women who are actively engaged in the good cause of improving life for themselves and others. In fact, the traditions in which I was reared support the ideals of eternal progression.

In a review of *Mormon Women Speak,* Richard Cummings asserts that the book "offers a refreshingly believable middle ground between the male-oriented preachiness of the collection of sermons by church authorities and the negativism of Sonia Johnson." For better or for worse, I seem to be occupying that middle ground. If this sounds less than courageous, I have to say that I have accepted the fact that the church is part of my body, and I am part of the church body. I feel that the church belongs as much to me as to anyone.

I don't claim that I fully understand either myself or other Mormon women, but my journey continues! It is an exciting one!

## Notes

1. Lowell L. Bennion, "Saint for All Seasons: An Interview with by Peggy Fletcher," *Sunstone* 10, no. 2 (February 1985): 18.

2. Wesley Johnson, "Editorial Preface," *Dialogue: A Journal of Mormon Thought* 1, no. 1 (Spring 1966): 4–5.

Also available from
GREG KOFFORD BOOKS

# Dead Wood and Rushing Water: Essays on Mormon Faith, Culture, and Family

## Boyd Jay Petersen

Paperback, ISBN: 978-1-58958-658-1

For over a decade, Boyd Petersen has been an active voice in Mormon studies and thought. In essays that steer a course between apologetics and criticism, striving for the balance of what Eugene England once called the "radical middle," he explores various aspects of Mormon life and culture—from the Dream Mine near Salem, Utah, to the challenges that Latter-day Saints of the millennial generation face today.

### Praise for *Dead Wood and Rushing Water*:

"*Dead Wood and Rushing Water* gives us a reflective, striving, wise soul ruminating on his world. In the tradition of Eugene England, Petersen examines everything in his Mormon life from the gold plates to missions to dream mines to doubt and on to Glenn Beck, Hugh Nibley, and gender. It is a book I had trouble putting down." — Richard L. Bushman, author of *Joseph Smith: Rough Stone Rolling*

"Boyd Petersen is correct when he says that Mormons have a deep hunger for personal stories—at least when they are as thoughtful and well-crafted as the ones he shares in this collection." — Jana Riess, author of *The Twible* and *Flunking Sainthood*

"Boyd Petersen invites us all to ponder anew the verities we hold, sharing in his humility, tentativeness, and cheerful confidence that our paths will converge in the end." — Terryl. L. Givens, author of *People of Paradox: A History of Mormon Culture*

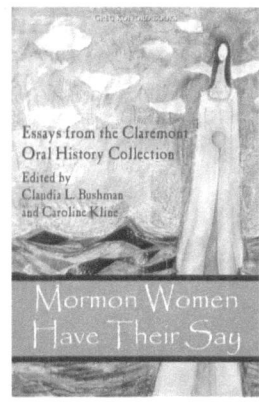

# Mormon Women Have Their Say: Essays from the Claremont Oral History Collection

## Edited by Claudia L. Bushman and Caroline Kline

Paperback, ISBN: 978-1-58958-494-5

The Claremont Women's Oral History Project has collected hundreds of interviews with Mormon women of various ages, experiences, and levels of activity. These interviews record the experiences of these women in their homes and family life, their church life, and their work life, in their roles as homemakers, students, missionaries, career women, single women, converts, and disaffected members. Their stories feed into and illuminate the broader narrative of LDS history and belief, filling in a large gap in Mormon history that has often neglected the lived experiences of women. This project preserves and perpetuates their voices and memories, allowing them to say share what has too often been left unspoken. The silent majority speaks in these records.

This volume is the first to explore the riches of the collection in print. A group of young scholars and others have used the interviews to better understand what Mormonism means to these women and what women mean for Mormonism. They explore those interviews through the lenses of history, doctrine, mythology, feminist theory, personal experience, and current events to help us understand what these women have to say about their own faith and lives.

**Praise for *Mormon Women Have Their Say*:**

"Using a variety of analytical techniques and their own savvy, the authors connect ordinary lives with enduring themes in Latter-day Saint faith and history." --Laurel Thatcher Ulrich, author of *Well-Behaved Women Seldom Make History*

"Essential. . . . In these pages, Mormon women will find *ourselves*." --Joanna Brooks, author of *The Book of Mormon Girl: A Memoir of an American Faith*

"The varieties of women's responses to the major issues in their lives will provide many surprises for the reader, who will be struck by how many different ways there are to be a thoughtful and faithful Latter-day Saint woman." --Armand Mauss, author of *All Abraham's Children: Changing Mormon Conceptions of Race and Lineage*

# Women at Church: Magnifying LDS Women's Local Impact

## Neylan McBaine

Paperback, ISBN: 978-1-58958-688-8

*Women at Church* is a practical and faithful guide to improving the way men and women work together at church. Looking at current administrative and cultural practices, the author explains why some women struggle with the gendered divisions of labor. She then examines ample real-life examples that are currently happening in local settings around the country that expand and reimagine gendered practices. Readers will understand how to evaluate possible pain points in current practices and propose solutions that continue to uphold all mandated church policies. Readers will be equipped with the tools they need to have respectful, empathetic and productive conversations about gendered practices in Church administration and culture.

**Praise for *Women at Church*:**

"Such a timely, faithful, and practical book! I suggest ordering this book in bulk to give to your bishopric, stake presidency, and all your local leadership to start a conversation on changing Church culture for women by letting our doctrine suggest creative local adaptations—Neylan McBaine shows the way!" — Valerie Hudson Cassler, author of *Women in Eternity, Women of Zion*

"A pivotal work replete with wisdom and insight. Neylan McBaine deftly outlines a workable programme for facilitating movement in the direction of the 'privileges and powers' promised the nascent Female Relief Society of Nauvoo." — Fiona Givens, co-author of *The God Who Weeps: How Mormonism Makes Sense of Life*

"In her timely and brilliant findings, Neylan McBaine issues a gracious invitation to rethink our assumptions about women's public Church service. Well researched, authentic, and respectful of the current Church administrative structure, McBaine shares exciting and practical ideas that address diverse needs and involve all members in the meaningful work of the Church." — Camille Fronk Olson, author of *Women of the Old Testament* and *Women of the New Testament*

# "Swell Suffering": A Biography of Maurine Whipple

## Veda Tebbs Hale

Paperback, ISBN: 978-1-58958-124-1
Hardcover, ISBN: 978-1-58958-122-7

Maurine Whipple, author of what some critics consider Mormonism's greatest novel, *The Giant Joshua,* is an enigma. Her prize-winning novel has never been out of print, and its portrayal of the founding of St. George draws on her own family history to produce its unforgettable and candid portrait of plural marriage's challenges. Yet Maurine's life is full of contradictions and unanswered questions. Veda Tebbs Hale, a personal friend of the paradoxical novelist, answers these questions with sympathy and tact, nailing each insight down with thorough research in Whipple's vast but under-utilized collected papers.

**Praise for *"Swell Suffering"*:**

"Hale achieves an admirable balance of compassion and objectivity toward an author who seemed fated to offend those who offered to love or befriend her. . . . Readers of this biography will be reminded that Whipple was a full peer of such Utah writers as Virginia Sorensen, Fawn Brodie, and Juanita Brooks, all of whom achieved national fame for their literary and historical works during the mid-twentieth century"
    —Levi S. Peterson, author of *The Backslider* and *Juanita Brooks: Mormon Historian*

# On the Road with Joseph Smith: An Author's Diary

## Richard L. Bushman

Paperback, ISBN 978-1-58958-102-9

After living with Joseph Smith for seven years and delivering the final proofs of his landmark study, *Joseph Smith: Rough Stone Rolling* to Knopf in July 2005, biographer Richard Lyman Bushman went "on the road" for a year, crisscrossing the country from coast to coast, delivering addresses on Joseph Smith and attending book-signings for the new biography.

Bushman confesses to hope and humility as he awaits reviews. He frets at the polarization that dismissed the book as either too hard on Joseph Smith or too easy. He yields to a very human compulsion to check sales figures on Amazon. com, but partway through the process stepped back with the recognition, "The book seems to be cutting its own path now, just as [I] hoped."

For readers coming to grips with the ongoing puzzle of the Prophet and the troublesome dimensions of their own faith, Richard Bushman, openly but not insistently presents himself as a believer. "I believe enough to take Joseph Smith seriously," he says. He draws comfort both from what he calls his "mantra" ("Today I will be a follower of Jesus Christ") and also from ongoing engagement with the intellectual challenges of explaining Joseph Smith.

**Praise for *On the Road With Joseph Smith*:**

"The diary is possibly unparalleled—an author of a recent book candidly dissecting his experiences with both Mormon and non-Mormon audiences . . . certainly deserves wider distribution—in part because it shows a talented historian laying open his vulnerabilities, and also because it shows how much any historian lays on the line when he writes about Joseph Smith."
　　　　　-Dennis Lythgoe, *Deseret News*

"By turns humorous and poignant, this behind-the-scenes look at Richard Bushman's public and private ruminations about Joseph Smith reveals a great deal—not only about the inner life of one of our greatest scholars, but about Mormonism at the dawn of the 21st century."
　　　　　-Jana Riess, co-author of *Mormonism for Dummies*

Common Ground—Different Opinions:
Latter-day Saints and Contemporary Issues

Edited by Justin F. White
and James E. Faulconer

Paperback, ISBN: 978-1-58958-573-7

There are many hotly debated issues about which many people disagree, and where common ground is hard to find. From evolution to environmentalism, war and peace to political partisanship, stem cell research to same-sex marriage, how we think about controversial issues affects how we interact as Latter-day Saints.

In this volume various Latter-day Saint authors address these and other issues from differing points of view. Though they differ on these tough questions, they have all found common ground in the gospel of Jesus Christ and the latter-day restoration. Their insights offer diverse points of view while demonstrating we can still love those with whom we disagree.

**Praise for *Common Ground—Different Opinions*:**

"[This book] provide models of faithful and diverse Latter-day Saints who remain united in the body of Christ. This collection clearly demonstrates that a variety of perspectives on a number of sensitive issues do in fact exist in the Church. . . . [T]he collection is successful in any case where it manages to give readers pause with regard to an issue they've been fond of debating, or convinces them to approach such conversations with greater charity and much more patience. It served as just such a reminder and encouragement to me, and for that reason above all, I recommend this book." — Blair Hodges, Maxwell Institute

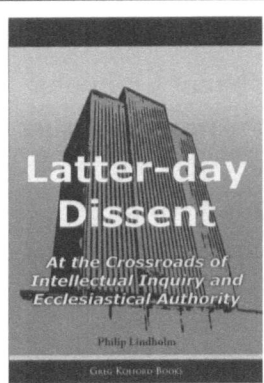

# Latter-Day Dissent:
## At the Crossroads of Intellectual Inquiry and Ecclesiastical Authority

### Philip Lindholm

Paperback, ISBN: 978-1-58958-128-9

This volume collects, for the first time in book form, stories from the "September Six," a group of intellectuals officially excommunicated or disfellowshipped from the LDS Church in September of 1993 on charges of "apostasy" or "conduct unbecoming" Church members. Their experiences are significant and yet are largely unknown outside of scholarly or more liberal Mormon circles, which is surprising given that their story was immediately propelled onto screens and cover pages across the Western world.

Interviews by Dr. Philip Lindholm (Ph.D. Theology, University of Oxford) include those of the "September Six," Lynne Kanavel Whitesides, Paul James Toscano, Maxine Hanks, Lavina Fielding Anderson, and D. Michael Quinn; as well as Janice Merrill Allred, Margaret Merrill Toscano, Thomas W. Murphy, and former employee of the LDS Church's Public Affairs Department, Donald B. Jessee.

Each interview illustrates the tension that often exists between the Church and its intellectual critics, and highlights the difficulty of accommodating congregational diversity while maintaining doctrinal unity—a difficulty hearkening back to the very heart of ancient Christianity.

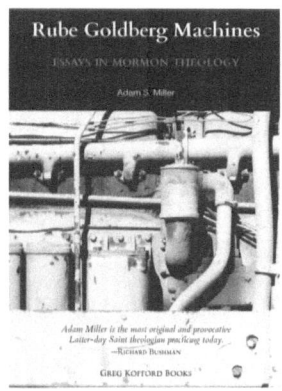

# Rube Goldberg Machines: Essays in Mormon Theology

## Adam S. Miller

Paperback, ISBN: 978-1-58958-193-7

"Adam Miller is the most original and provocative Latter-day Saint theologian practicing today."

—Richard Bushman, author of *Joseph Smith: Rough Stone Rolling*

"As a stylist, Miller gives Nietzsche a run for his money. As a believer, Miller is as submissive as Augustine hearing a child's voice in the garden. Miller is a theologian of the ordinary, thinking about our ordinary beliefs in very non-ordinary ways while never insisting that the ordinary become extra-ordinary."

—James Faulconer, Richard L. Evans Chair of Religious Understanding,Brigham Young University

"Miller's language is both recognizably Mormon and startlingly original. . . . The whole is an essay worthy of the name, inviting the reader to try ideas, following the philosopher pilgrim's intellectual progress through tangled brambles and into broad fields, fruitful orchards, and perhaps a sacred grove or two."

—Kristine Haglund, editor of *Dialogue: A Journal of Mormon Thought*

"Miller's Rube Goldberg theology is nothing like anything done in the Mormon tradition before."

—Blake Ostler, author of the EXPLORING MORMON THOUGHT series

"The value of Miller's writings is in the modesty he both exhibits and projects onto the theological enterprise, even while showing its joyfully disruptive potential. Conventional Mormon minds may not resonate with every line of poetry and provocation—but Miller surely afflicts the comfortable, which is the theologian's highest end."

—Terryl Givens, author of *By the Hand of Mormon: The American Scripture that Launched a New World Religion*

# For Zion:
# A Mormon Theology of Hope

## Joseph M. Spencer

Paperback, ISBN: 978-1-58958-568-3

What is hope? What is Zion? And what does it mean to hope for Zion? In this insightful book, Joseph Spencer explores these questions through the scriptures of two continents separated by nearly two millennia. In the first half, Spencer engages in a rich study of Paul's letter to the Roman to better understand how the apostle understood hope and what it means to have it. In the second half of the book, Spencer jumps to the early years of the Restoration and the various revelations on consecration to understand how Latter-day Saints are expected to strive for Zion. Between these halves is an interlude examining the hoped-for Zion that both thrived in the Book of Mormon and was hoped to be established again.

**Praise for *For Zion*:**

"Joseph Spencer is one of the most astute readers of sacred texts working in Mormon Studies. Blending theological savvy, historical grounding, and sensitive readings of scripture, he has produced an original and compelling case for consecration and the life of discipleship." — Terryl Givens, author, *Wrestling the Angel: The Foundations of Mormon Thought*

"*For Zion: A Mormon Theology of Hope* is more than a theological reflection. It also consists of able textual exegesis, historical contextualization, and philosophic exploration. Spencer's careful readings of Paul's focus on hope in Romans and on Joseph Smith's development of consecration in his early revelations, linking them as he does with the Book of Mormon, have provided an intriguing, intertextual avenue for understanding what true stewardship should be for us—now and in the future. As such he has set a new benchmark for solid, innovative Latter-day Saint scholarship that is at once provocative and challenging." — Eric D. Huntsman, author, *The Miracles of Jesus*